Best Easy Day Hikes
Indianapolis

Help Us Keep This Guide Up to Date

Every effort has been made by the author and editors to make this guide as accurate and useful as possible. However, many things can change after a guide is published—trails are rerouted, regulations change, techniques evolve, facilities come under new management, etc.

We appreciate hearing from you concerning your experiences with this guide and how you feel it could be improved and kept up to date. While we may not be able to respond to all comments and suggestions, we'll take them to heart and we'll also make certain to share them with the author. Please send your comments and suggestions to the following address:

FalconGuides
Reader Response/Editorial Department
246 Goose Lane, Suite 200
Guilford, CT 06437

Thanks for your input, and happy trails!

Best Easy Day Hikes Series

Best Easy Day Hikes
Indianapolis

Kat Green and Kayla Woodward

FALCONGUIDES

GUILFORD, CONNECTICUT

FALCONGUIDES®

An imprint of The Rowman & Littlefield Publishing Group, Inc.
4501 Forbes Blvd., Ste. 200
Lanham, MD 20706
www.rowman.com
Falcon and FalconGuides are registered trademarks and Make Adventure Your Story is a trademark of The Rowman & Littlefield Publishing Group, Inc.

Distributed by NATIONAL BOOK NETWORK

Copyright © 2021 The Rowman & Littlefield Publishing Group, Inc.
Hike descriptions originally published in *Best Hikes Near Indianapolis* by Nick Werner © 2012, fully updated and revised by Kat Green and Kayla Woodward.
Photos by Kayla Woodward
Maps by Melissa Baker

British Library Cataloguing in Publication Information available

Library of Congress Cataloging-in-Publication Data

Names: Green, Kat, 1990- author. | Woodward, Kayla, author.
Title: Best easy day hikes Indianapolis / Kat Green and Kayla Woodward.
Description: Guilford, Connecticut : FalconGuides, 2021. | Summary: "Best Easy Day Hikes Indianapolis includes concise descriptions and detailed maps for nineteen easy-to-follow trails, for an accessible range of abilities"— Provided by publisher.
Identifiers: LCCN 2020040148 (print) | LCCN 2020040149 (ebook) | ISBN 9781493055883 (trade paperback) | ISBN 9781493055890 (epub)
Subjects: LCSH: Hiking—Indiana—Indianapolis Region—Guidebooks. | Trails—Indiana—Indianapolis Region—Guidebooks. | Indianapolis Region (Ind.) —Guidebooks.
Classification: LCC GV199.42.I62 I644 2021 (print) | LCC GV199.42.I62 (ebook) | DDC 796.5109772/52—dc23
LC record available at https://lccn.loc.gov/2020040148
LC ebook record available at https://lccn.loc.gov/2020040149

∞™ The paper used in this publication meets the minimum requirements of American National Standard for Information Sciences—Permanence of Paper for Printed Library Materials, ANSI/NISO Z39.48-1992.

Contents

Acknowledgments

As coauthors of this publication, we would like to first thank the original stewards of the land that we currently call Indiana for caring for, protecting, and loving this region since time immemorial: the Miami, the Delaware, the Potawatomi, the Shawnee, the Kickapoo, the Winnebago, the Wea, the Wyandotte, the Ottawa, the Chippewa, the Menominee, the Fox, the Sauk, the Creek, and others whose names history failed to remember. We would also like to thank the current establishments in place that work to protect, maintain, and improve these natural spaces.

From Kayla Woodward: Thank you to my husband and hiking buddy, Robert, for spending so much time on the trail with me for research for this book.

From Kat Green: Thank you to my dad for nurturing my love for the outdoors from a young age, to my partner, Jevon, for listening enthusiastically to every paragraph I read aloud to you, and thank you to my coauthor, Kayla, without whom none of this would have been possible.

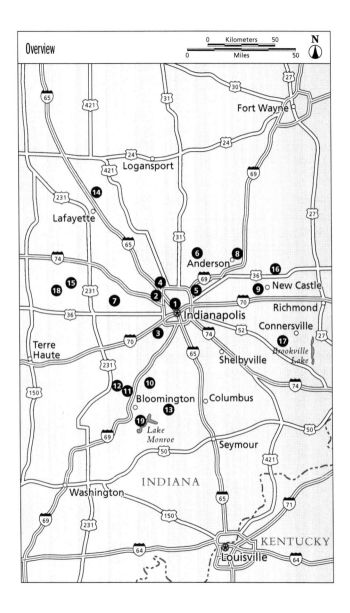

Overview

Kilometers
0   50

Miles
0   50

N

Fort Wayne

Logansport

Lafayette

Anderson

Indianapolis

New Castle

Richmond

Connersville

Brookville Lake

Terre Haute

Shelbyville

Bloomington

Columbus

Lake Monroe

Seymour

Washington

INDIANA

KENTUCKY

Louisville

Introduction

Indiana does not have a reputation for its outdoor recreation opportunities. The state sits in a section of the country that is seemingly unremarkable. However, with a closer look, hikers can find more than a few unique gems within the Hoosier State. Ranging from high canyon walls to cultural discovery, this guide will take you through some of the most stunning natural areas within central Indiana. It doesn't matter if you're an avid hiking enthusiast, a beginner with a new pair of hiking boots, a local, or an out-of-towner. The areas highlighted here will leave you with a newfound appreciation for this little "flyover" state.

We chose the nineteen hikes in this book to offer something for every type of hiker. Please note that the term "easy" is relative. Read each hike description in detail to make sure it's right for you. These trails will take you through wide prairies, canyons of sandstone and limestone, rich hardwood forests, floodplains, swamps, vast lakes, meandering rivers, hilltops, and ravine bottoms. Most of these trails will also give hikers the opportunity to connect and learn about the land's cultural and ecological history along the way. Those who take the time to learn the history and conservation surrounding these natural spaces will almost certainly become better stewards of the land.

Another important aspect of these hikes is their proximity to Indianapolis. We wanted to offer recreational options for those just getting off work as well as those with a long weekend and everything in between. While all of the hikes listed can be completed within a day (including travel time from Indianapolis), there are some areas that hikers may want to explore further and are highly encouraged to do so.

Additionally, the length and time commitments of these trails are widely varied. Those looking for an endurance experience and those seeking an afternoon stroll have plenty of options.

Weather

Central Indiana has a humid continental climate that results in cold winters, hot damp summers, and mostly pleasant spring and fall seasons. The best months for hiking are typically April, May, June, September, and October. Those who venture out during this time can be rewarded with mild temperatures and stunning seasonal color changes. However, be aware that seasonal rains that come in spring and fall significantly affect many landscapes within this book. While precipitation is fairly consistent throughout the seasons, May tends to be the rainiest month of the year. Spring also brings a more significant chance of thunderstorms, floods, and tornadoes. Fall tends to be less humid and dryer than the other months, but thunderstorms and significant rainfall are not out of the question. If you choose to hike during these times be prepared by understanding the terrain you're entering, checking the weather, bringing wet weather gear with you, and consulting park staff about trail conditions before you go if possible.

The average daytime temperatures for central Indiana during spring and fall range from 60 to 80 degrees Fahrenheit while nighttime temperatures range from 30 to 50 degrees Fahrenheit. Summer months can soar to temperatures above 100 degrees Fahrenheit while winter months typically drop into the low teens, but can see negative numbers. Indianapolis winters see an average of 22 inches of snowfall per year, providing some winter recreation opportunities. Those who venture out into the snow should be prepared for heavy snow and icy conditions. Whatever the season, be sure to bring plenty of water. The humidity of this region will require you to hydrate accordingly.

Flora & Fauna

Throughout its history, much of central Indiana has been deforested for urban expansion and agricultural needs. Before the time of European settlers, nearly all of central Indiana was blanketed in its native hardwood forests and prairies, but by 1917 that once vast region had been reduced to 7 percent of its original glory. Thankfully, that figure has grown to around 20 percent and is continuing to grow. The dotting of protected natural areas provide a refuge for central Indiana's flora and fauna to flourish.

Ninety-five percent of Indiana's forests are classified as deciduous hardwood forests and are mostly made up of hickory, maple, oak, sycamore, and beech. Forests made up mostly of beech and maple trees tend to be found in the plains of Indiana due to the higher moisture content, as compared to the oak and hickory forests that prefer the well-drained hills of steeper areas. Floodplains typically host cottonwoods and sycamores but most of Indiana's forests house a healthy mixture of these hardwoods.

In the spring, central Indiana offers a variety of radiant wildflowers such as spring butterfly milkweed and Virginia bluebells but it's also home to some not-so-friendly species: poison ivy and stinging nettle. Poison ivy can be found just about everywhere but thankfully it's easy to identify by its dark, glossy, and droopy leaves of three with a woody stem. Stinging nettle is typically found near moisture and is easily avoidable if you're paying attention.

As for fauna, central Indiana is home to a diverse array of woodland creatures. Whitetail deer, coyotes, racoons, cottontail rabbits, Indiana bats, chipmunks, and grey squirrels are fairly common sights if you find yourself in the woods often enough. Foxes and bobcats, while plentiful, are rare and lucky sights. Sadly, the native black bears and cougars of this area were eradicated due to over hunting before the turn of the twentieth century, however, some research shows these species may be migrating back into the region, though there's no significant evidence to date. With all of that said, the most concerning creatures to worry about in Indiana's forests, in our opinion, are ticks. It's advisable to wear long pants and a hat, and to be cautious of laying your gear down in areas of dense vegetation. Unless it's the dead of winter, it's a good idea to check yourself and your partners for ticks after each outing.

Preparing for the Hike

Regardless of the duration or distance of the hike, it's important to be well prepared. At best, it will provide a much more enjoyable hike, and at worst you'll have what you need for an emergency. Proper footwear is important. Some of the hikes in this book are probably doable with a standard pair of tennis shoes while others require better ankle support. For all of these hikes, having proper layers is important. Have a warmer layer with you as well as rain gear in the event of inclement weather. Always be sure to bring plenty of water, no matter the season, and actually hydrate yourself. During the warmer months bug repellant in this region may make you more comfortable as well, especially when hiking near water. Be sure to inform someone of your plans before heading out.

Wilderness Restrictions and Regulations

In this book, outdoor recreational areas fall into the following categories: state forests, national forests, nature preserves, state parks, and municipal parks. State parks and some municipal parks require an entry fee, while the other public land areas may be free to access and don't require a permit. Operating hours vary from area to area, but most state, city, town, and county parks, as well as nature preserves, limit recreation to daylight hours. State and national forests allow nighttime usage unless otherwise posted, but all activities are at the user's own risk.

Hunting is prominent in this region and allowed in state and national forests. Hikers should be aware of hunting seasons before entering these areas. The only warmer months that are free of hunters are June and July. Foraging is permitted in Hoosier National Forest and state-owned areas, excluding nature preserves.

Please note, however, that in Hoosier National Forest, digging plants is not allowed and collecting ginseng and goldenseal is prohibited on both Hoosier National Forest and state properties. Contact the public land's management for more information on gathering natural materials.

Leave No Trace

We, as trail users and advocates, must be especially vigilant to make sure our passage leaves no lasting mark. Here are some basic guidelines for preserving trails in the region:

- Pack out all your own trash, including biodegradable items like orange peels. You might also pack out garbage left by less considerate hikers.

- Don't approach or feed any wild creatures—the ground squirrel eyeing your snack food is best able to survive if it remains self-reliant.

- Don't pick wildflowers or gather rocks, antlers, feathers, and other treasures along the trail. Removing these items will only take away from the next hiker's experience.

- Avoid damaging trailside soils and plants by remaining on the established route. This is also a good rule of thumb for avoiding poison ivy and briars.

- Don't cut switchbacks, which can promote erosion.

- Be courteous by not making loud noises while hiking.

- Some of these trails are multi-use, which means you'll share them with other hikers, joggers, mountain bikers, and equestrians. Familiarize yourself with the proper trail etiquette, yielding the trail when appropriate.

- Use outhouses at trailheads or along the trail.

How to Use This Guide

This guide contains just about everything you'll ever need to choose, plan for, enjoy, and survive a hike near Indianapolis. *Best Easy Day Hikes Near Indianapolis* features nineteen hikes with maps and directions. Here's an outline of the book's major components:

The three chapters are organized by the length of travel time from Indianapolis to the trailhead. Chapter One encompasses hikes that are in and around Indianapolis, generally less than half an hour away. Chapter Two is composed of hikes that are within an hour's drive of Indianapolis, and Chapter Three is made up of hikes that are over an hour of travel time from Indianapolis. Each hike starts with a short summary of the trail's highlights. These quick overviews give you an idea of the trail's character.

Following the overview you'll find the hike specs: quick overview details of the hike. Most are self-explanatory, but here are some details on others:

Distance: The total distance of the listed route—one-way for loop hikes, round-trip on an out-and-back or lollipop hike, point-to-point for a shuttle. Marked and unmarked options are additional.

Hiking time: The average time it will take to cover the route. This is based on the total distance, elevation gain, and condition and difficulty of the trail. Your fitness level will also affect your time.

Difficulty: Each hike has been assigned a level of difficulty. The hikes in this book are all considered easy by the authors but "easy" is a relative term. **Be sure to read the details of each hike to make sure it's right for you and your abilities.** These levels are meant to be a guideline only and the hike may prove easier or harder for different people depending on ability and fitness level.

- **Easy**—Minimal hilly terrain; smooth-surfaced dirt or gravel trail. Distances for easy routes are also usually less than 3 miles.
- **Moderate**—Moderate hilly terrain and potentially rough/uneven terrain. Distances vary.
- **More Difficult**—Several areas of hilly terrain and rough and/or rocky terrain. Distances vary though length is taken into consideration when assigning a difficulty rating. No trail in the book exceeds 11 miles.

Trail surface: A general overview of terrain and features.

Best season: The authors' opinion of the best season to hike that specific trail based on experience.

Other trail users: Gives hikers an idea of who to expect while on the trail.

Canine compatibility: Information regarding pet regulations for each trail. It's a good idea to seek this information before hiking as updates do occur. Additionally, make sure each hike is appropriate for your dog. Some trails in this book may not be.

Fees and permits: Whether fees are charged for entry to this trail or area or not. Fees often change and so specific monetary amounts are not included in this book.

Maps: Information regarding where to find maps of each trail.

Trail contact: Information regarding who to contact about trail information.

Finding the trailhead: Directions to the trailhead from downtown Indianapolis.

The Hike: This section provides more detailed information about what you can expect to find while hiking each trail.

It offers information regarding landmarks, ecosystems, and the overall hike experience.

History: This section offers a brief overview of the history of each trail or park that can help provide context to the areas of the trail.

Miles and Directions: Mileage cues identify each turn and trail name change. Options are provided occasionally and can be used to shorten or elongate the trail.

Trail Finder

Hike	Best Hikes for Geology Lovers	Best Hikes for Water Lovers	Best Hikes for Adventure Lovers	Best Hikes for Cultural Education	Best Hikes for Children	Best Hikes for After Work	Best Hikes for Wildlife Viewing
1. Monon Rail Trail							
2. Eagle Creek Park: Blue Trail							
3. Sodalis Nature Park						▪	
4. Starkey Park Loop						▪	
5. Fort Harrison State Park: Fall Creek/ Camp Creek Trails						▪	
6. Strawtown Koteewi Park: Northern and Southern Trail Loops				▪			

Hike	Best Hikes for Geology Lovers	Best Hikes for Water Lovers	Best Hikes for Adventure Lovers	Best Hikes for Cultural Education	Best Hikes for Children	Best Hikes for After Work	Best Hikes for Wildlife Viewing
7. McCloud Nature Park Loop		■				■	
8. Mounds State Park: Trail 5		■		■		■	
9. Westwood Park: Mountain Biking/Hiking Trail		■	■				■
10. Morgan-Monroe State Forest: Low Gap Trail			■				
11. Beanblossom Bottoms Nature Preserve		■			■		■
12. McCormick's Creek State Park: Trail 5	■						

Hike	Best Hikes for Geology Lovers	Best Hikes for Water Lovers	Best Hikes for Adventure Lovers	Best Hikes for Cultural Education	Best Hikes for Children	Best Hikes for After Work	Best Hikes for Wildlife Viewing
13. Brown County State Park: CCC Trail (Trail 2)				■			
14. Prophetstown State Park: Loop Trail		■		■			■
15. Shades State Park: Western Ravines Loop	■	■	■				
16. Summit Lake State Park: Prairie Trail					■		■
17. Mary Gray Bird Sanctuary							■

Hike	Best Hikes for Geology Lovers	Best Hikes for Water Lovers	Best Hikes for Adventure Lovers	Best Hikes for Cultural Education	Best Hikes for Children	Best Hikes for After Work	Best Hikes for Wildlife Viewing
18. Turkey Run State Park: Rocky Hollow-Falls Canyon Nature Preserve	∙	∙	∙				
19. Hoosier National Forest: Pate Hollow			∙				∙

Map Legend

═══⬡65⬡═══	Interstate Highway
───⬡52⬡───	US Highway
───⬡37⬡───	State Highway
───▭232▭───	County Road
──────────	Local Road
▰▰▰▰▰▰▰▰▰	Featured Trail
‐ ‐ ‐ ‐ ‐ ‐	Trail
──────────	Paved Trail
┝┼┼┼┼┼┼┥	Railroad
〜〜〜〜〜	River/Creek
⬭	Body of Water
‖‖‖	Boardwalk
⛵	Boat Launch
⏝	Bridge
▲	Camping
⌒	Cave
•—•	Gate
❷	Information Center
🅿	Parking
▲	Peak
⛩	Picnic Area
■	Point of Interest/Structure
⊞	Restroom
🗼	Tower
○	Town
❶	Trailhead
⧉	Viewpoint/Overlook
≋	Waterfall

In Town: Trails Closest to Indianapolis

1 Monon Rail Trail

This trail guides you through a hidden natural oasis just minutes from downtown. Stretching from the east edge of downtown Indianapolis to the town of Westfield, the Monon Rail Trail offers multiple start and end points, giving its users the ability to choose their own adventure. This mostly flat and paved trail connects dozens of neighborhoods, leading you over canals, by culturally significant sites, and around the artistic expressions of downtown areas.

Distance: 2.6-mile out-and-back
Hiking time: 1–1.5 hours
Difficulty: Easy due to flat terrain
Trail surface: Flat, asphalt, mostly smooth surface along entire route
Best season: Mar to Nov; heavy multi-use traffic on weekends in warmer months
Other trail users: Joggers, bikers, rollerbladers, skateboarders

Canine compatibility: Leashed dogs permitted
Fees and permits: None
Schedule: Daily, dawn to dusk, year-round
Maps: No route maps available, but route can be viewed on Google Maps.
Trail contact: Indy Parks and Recreation, 200 E Washington St., Suite 2301, Indianapolis 46204; (317) 327-7275

Finding the trailhead: From downtown Indianapolis travel north on Meridian Street for 8.5 miles. Turn right onto East 75th Street and travel 0.9 mile; parking is available on the right about 400 feet from the trailhead. GPS: N39 89.04' / W86 14.08'

The Hike

From the trailhead at East 75th Street, head south toward the city of Broad Ripple. This section of the Monon begins by bordering Marott Park, before crossing over the White River and entering into Broad Ripple. To complete this segment, turn around at the intersection with the Central Canal Towpath before the Monon crosses over the Central Canal and return to the intersection of 75th Street. Distance can easily be added to the hike by continuing straight along the Monon Trail as far south as East 10th Street downtown, as far north as Westfield at 176th Street and turning around at any point, or turning right onto the Central Canal Towpath through Broad Ripple. There are also various trails through Marott Park which can be accessed from the Monon. The length of the trail is mostly straight and flat, with occasional street crossings. Some street crossings take the form of crosswalks—be sure to watch for vehicle traffic—and some take the form of bridges underneath or above the street. Always stay to the right side of the trail, as bike traffic will pass on your left. Major destinations or entrance points include Broad Ripple, the Indiana State Fairgrounds, Carmel Arts and Culture District, and Grand Park in Westfield. Many connector trails offer alternate routes such as the Indianapolis Cultural Trail to downtown, the Fall Creek Trail, the Central Canal Towpath through Broad Ripple, the Eagle Creek Trail toward Eagle Creek Park, the Midland Trace Trail in Westfield, and the Monon North Trail that extends farther north toward Sheridan.

History

The word "Monon" is derived from words in the Potawa-tomi language that early settlers heard as "metamonong" or "monong," which seemed to mean "tote" or "swift running." From 1847 to 1971 the Monon Railroad was a popular rail-road line connecting Chicago and Indianapolis, with stops at major cities and towns along its route. After the decline of rail travel and the sale of the company in 1987, portions of the line were abandoned. The first portions of the Monon Rail Trail were created in the late 1990s, and the project has continued to grow throughout the state in the decades since. Today the trail has segments in northwest Indiana in Ham-mond, the segment running from Westfield to downtown Indianapolis, and a segment that extends north from West-field to Sheridan.

Miles and Directions

0.0   Start from the intersection of East 75th Street and head south along the paved Monon Trail.

0.3   At the junction with an unmarked Marott Park trail, continue straight on the paved Monon Trail.

0.5   At the junction with an unmarked Marott Park trail, continue straight on the paved Monon Trail.

0.7   At the junction with an unmarked Marott Park trail, continue straight on the bridge across the White River.

1.3   At the intersection with the Canal Towpath, turn around and head back north.

1.8   Continue straight across the bridge over the White River.

1.9   At the junction with an unmarked Marott Park trail, continue straight.

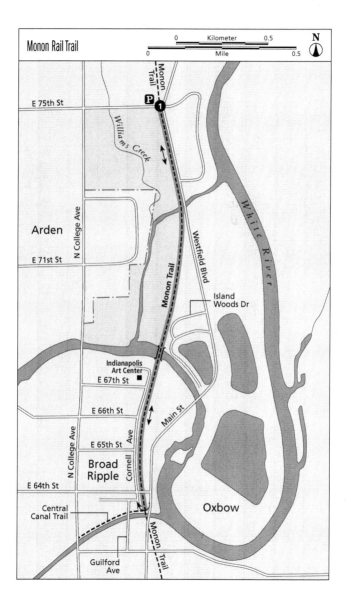

Monon Rail Trail

| 0 | Kilometer | 0.5 |

| 0 | Mile | 0.5 |

N

Monon Trail

E 75th St

Williams Creek

Arden

N College Ave

E 71st St

Monon Trail

Westfield Blvd

White River

Island
Woods Dr

Indianapolis
Art Center

E 67th St

E 66th St

Main St

N College Ave

E 65th St

Cornell Ave

Broad
Ripple

E 64th St

Oxbow

Central
Canal Trail

Monon Trail

Guilford Ave

2.2 At the junction with an unmarked Marott Park trail, continue straight on the paved Monon Trail.

2.3 At the junction with an unmarked Marott Park trail, continue straight on the paved Monon Trail.

2.6 Arrive at the trailhead and turn left to return to the parking area.

2 Eagle Creek Park: Blue Trail

Eagle Creek's stunning reservoir encircled by forests and wildlife provides the perfect after work or weekend retreat in the midst of the city's westside neighborhoods. This trail begins in a hilly forest and leads hikers around the perimeter of the reservoir's bird sanctuary. Bald eagles can often be spotted in and around the sanctuary before the trail curves back into the woods toward the trailhead.

Distance: 2.8-mile loop
Hiking time: 1.5–2.5 hours
Difficulty: Moderate due to mild terrain
Trail surface: Crushed gravel and packed dirt, short steep hills with exposed roots
Best season: May through Apr during bird migration season
Other trail users: Joggers, bird watchers, fishers

Canine compatibility: Leashed dogs permitted
Fees and permits: Entrance fee charged
Schedule: Daily, dawn to dusk. Gates close promptly at dusk.
Maps: Available at gate houses and the Earth Discovery Center
Trail contact: Eagle Creek Park, 7840 W 56th St., Indianapolis 46254; (317) 327-7110; https://eaglecreekpark.org

Finding the trailhead: From downtown Indianapolis take I-65 N to West 71st Street in Pike Township. Take exit 124 for 71st Street. Turn left onto 71st Street and continue onto Eagle Creek Parkway. After you pass the north gate entrance, park in the 71st Street parking lot on the right. You can start the loop going east (across the road from the parking lot, away from the bird sanctuary), or west (same side of the road as the parking lot, toward the bird sanctuary). GPS: N39 52.61' / W86 17.70'

The Hike

This trail begins at the Blue Trail trailhead and wraps through classic midwestern forests while weaving up and down a few mild hills. Throughout the first 1.2 miles, this trail crosses multiple trail junctions and roads. When in doubt, follow signs for the Blue Trail. At about mile 1.4, the trail begins to travel around the outer edge of the bird sanctuary. Nearly half of this trail leads around the bird sanctuary portion of the Eagle Creek Reservoir providing great wildlife viewing opportunities. Note that trail activities such as swimming, boating, and fishing are not allowed within the bird sanctuary. Bald eagles can often be seen flying overhead, fishing, or perched in trees along the shoreline. There are usually one to four bald eagles living in the area, however they may migrate south if the water freezes solid during the winter months. Good spots to watch for eagles include the Eagle Creek Ornithology Center, the marina, and anywhere with a wide view of the sky and shoreline along the reservoir. The Blue Trail connects with the Red Trail in various places, allowing for extended hike options. Shortly after leaving the water's edge around mile 2.5, the trail leads back to the trailhead.

History

Eagle Creek Reservoir was originally dammed in 1966 following a serious flood in 1957, which caused considerable damage across the west side of Marion County. In 1972, Eagle Creek Park was officially opened as the fourth largest municipal park in the nation, and it remains one of the largest today. It has seen continuous growth in its conservation and recreation efforts including Eagle Crest Nature Preserve, the bird sanctuary, and a world-class rowing course for the

Eagle Creek Park: Blue Trail

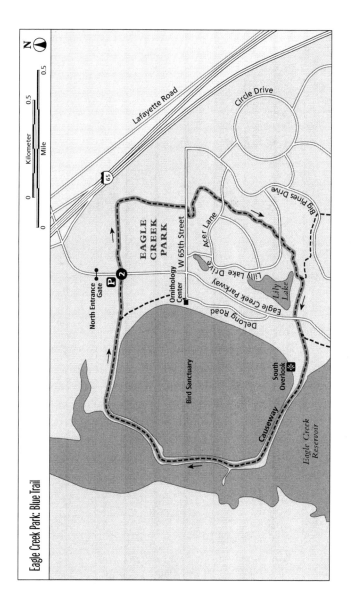

1987 Pan American Games. Be sure to check out the board on the south side of the Ornithology Center to see which birds have recently been spotted in the park.

Miles and Directions

0.0 Start from the Blue Trail trailhead in the 71st Street parking lot just after the northern entry gate, on the eastern side of Eagle Creek Parkway.

0.1 At the junction with the Red Trail, continue straight, following the signs for the Blue Trail.

0.3 At the junction with the Green Trail, continue straight following markers for the Blue Trail.

0.5 Continue straight crossing over paved road West 65th Street, following the crosswalk.

0.7 Continue straight crossing over paved road Acer Lane, following the crosswalk.

0.9 Continue straight crossing over paved road Lilly Lake Drive, following the crosswalk.

1.1 At the junction with the Red Trail, keep right following signs for the Blue Trail.

1.2 Continue straight crossing paved road Eagle Creek Parkway, following the crosswalk.

1.3 At the junction with the Red and Edesess Trails, continue straight, following signs for the Blue Trail.

1.4 At the junction with the Edesess Trail, continue straight downhill toward the reservoir, following signs for the Blue Trail.

2.5 At the junction with the Red Trail, continue straight, following signs for the Blue Trail.

2.6 Continue straight toward 71st Street, past the unmarked trail. Turning right here will take you to the park's Ornithology Center.

2.8 Arrive back at the trailhead and parking lot.

3 Sodalis Nature Park

This trail guides hikers around a humble nature park, which exists to protect the endangered Indiana bat *Myotis sodalis*. You will find gentle, even terrain along this loop as it connects multiple trails marked by symbols on wooden posts. This casual trail gives its users an insight to Indiana's ecosystem while also providing an enjoyable walk in the woods.

Distance: 2.3-mile loop

Hiking time: 1–2 hours

Difficulty: Easy due to mild terrain

Trail surface: Crushed gravel and packed dirt; occasional wooden bridge can be slippery

Best season: Trail is open year-round, with less foot traffic in the winter months. The endangered Indiana bat, *Myotis sodalis*, roosts along Bat Haven Trail in the warmer months of the year and may be spotted feeding around sunset.

Other trail users: Joggers, fishers

Canine compatibility: Leashed dogs permitted

Fees and permits: None

Schedule: Open year-round, dawn to dusk

Maps: No trail maps available; trails marked with wooden signposts.

Trail contact: Town of Plainfield Department of Public Works, 986 S Center Street Plainfield 46168; (317) 839-3490

Finding the trailhead: From downtown Indianapolis, take I-70 W. In 13.1 miles take exit 66 toward Mooresville. Turn left onto IN 267 S. In 1.1 miles turn left onto East County Road 750 S. In 1.2 miles turn right onto South County Road 975 E; the destination will be on your right. GPS N39 64.99' / W86 34.95'

The Hike

This trail takes hikers around the perimeter of the park and through a 210-acre nature preserve that was established to protect the endangered Indiana bat. The loop begins from the parking area on the Oak Trace Trail, leading hikers around the eastern shore of the fishing pond. This trail leads down a mixture of crushed gravel paths, singletrack natural surfaces, and a few slippery wooden bridges surrounded mostly by a healthy hardwood forest. Around mile 1.2 the Oak Trace Trail will become Bat Haven Trail. As hikers move through the mature forest, look around at the tree trunks for human-made bat roosts. During the warmer months, the endangered Indiana bat (*Myotis sodalis*) roosts in this area. Please give these creatures their space and do not approach these roosts on your hike. As this section loops back around to the east, it provides serene glimpses of small waterways along the way. This area is a floodplain forest so be aware of wet weather that could cause muddy trail conditions. At around mile 1.9, the trail makes a brief connection with the Beaver Ridge Trail in order to reconnect with the Oak Trace Trail that will guide hikers back around the fishing pond and to the trailhead.

History

Sodalis Nature Park exists within a permanently protected 210-acre conservation area that was established to protect the endangered Indiana bat (*Myotis sodalis*). This park was created from a collaboration between Hendricks County Parks and Recreation, the Indianapolis Airport Authority, and the US Fish and Wildlife Service. In 2019, the park transitioned ownership from Hendricks County Parks to

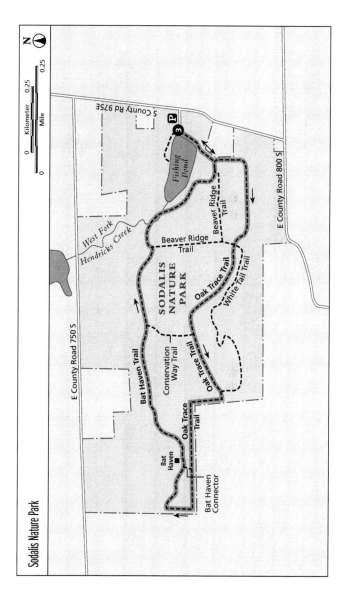

Sodalis Nature Park

N

0   Kilometer   0.25
0   Mile   0.25

E County Road 750 S

West Fork Hendricks Creek

SODALIS NATURE PARK

Bat Haven Trail

Bat Haven

Conservation Way Trail

Oak Trace Trail

Bat Haven Connector

Oak Trace Trail

Beaver Ridge Trail

Oak Trace Trail

White Tail Trail

Beaver Ridge Trail

Fishing Pond

S County Rd 975E

E County Road 800 S

P

3

the Town of Plainfield as a result of a larger land purchase, encompassing 1,800 acres. The Town of Plainfield plans to create a larger regional park while maintaining its protections for the Indiana bat.

Miles and Directions

0.0 Start on the Oak Trace Trail from Sodalis Nature Park parking area, leading to the left of the fishing pond.

0.1 At the trail junction with Beaver Ridge, stay left for the Oak Trace Trail.

0.4 Continue straight on the Oak Trace Trail at the four-way intersection with the White Tail Trail.

0.6 Continue straight for the Oak Trace Trail at the junction with the Conservation Way Trail on the right.

1.0 Continue straight at the junction with the Bat Haven connector trail on the right.

1.2 Turn right as the Oak Trace Trail ends and becomes the Bat Haven Trail.

1.3 Continue straight at the junction with the Bat Haven connector trail on the right.

1.7 Continue straight on the Bat Haven Trail at the junction with the Conservation Way Trail on the right.

1.9 At the T intersection, turn left on the Beaver Ridge Trail.

2.1 Turn left, back onto the Oak Trace Trail toward the fishing pond.

2.2 Stay left on Oak Trace Trail, continuing toward the pond and parking area.

2.3 Arrive back at the trailhead and parking area.

4 Starkey Park Loop

This trail system sits just southwest of downtown Zionsville, providing a hidden gem in this growing Indianapolis suburb. The trail begins by descending from the residential area above into the riparian zone along Eagle Creek below. The loop connects six well-marked trails within the Starkey Park trail system as it leads hikers around the perimeter of the park before ending with a moderate climb back to the trailhead.

Distance: 2-mile loop
Hiking time: 1–1.5 hours
Difficulty: Moderate due to multiple steep staircases
Trail surface: Natural surface singletrack, crushed gravel
Best season: Late spring for wildflower season, fall for changing leaves
Other trail users: Joggers, fishers
Canine compatibility: Leashed dogs permitted
Fees and permits: None

Schedule: Daily from sunrise to sunset, year-round
Maps: No park maps available; metal signs showing the route can be found at the parking area and various points throughout the park.
Trail contact: Zionsville Parks Department, 1075 Parkway Dr., Zionsville 46077; (317) 722-2273; www.zionsville-in.gov/parks

Finding the trailhead: From downtown Indianapolis, take I-65 N and continue for 9.2 miles to exit 123 for I-465 N. After 2.8 miles take exit 23 for 86th Street, then turn left. Continue 1.1 miles, then turn right onto Moore Road. Continue for 1 mile, then turn right onto West 96th Street. Continue for 0.6 mile, then turn left onto Ford Road. Continue for 1.1 miles. Turn right onto Starkey Avenue. Continue for 0.3 mile. Turn right onto Sugarbush Drive and continue for 0.1 mile. Look for signs for the park on your left. GPS: N39 56.49' / W86 16.30'

The Hike

Starkey Park offers 3.43 miles of trails just southwest of downtown Zionsville and less than half an hour north of downtown Indianapolis. This hike includes Starkey Park Trails 1, 2, 3, 4, 5, and Eagle Creek Trail 1 to form a 2-mile perimeter loop. Main trail junctions are marked with metal directional guides displaying a map of the trails. When in doubt stay straight for this trail, but this park is easy to navigate, even without a map. The hike begins above a steep ravine that you'll quickly descend into via a metal staircase. Once in the bottom of the ravine, the trail enters a riparian ecosystem as it nears Eagle Creek. The surrounding floodplain woods are comprised largely of sycamore, maple, and cottonwood trees while the underbrush is thick with stinging nettle. It's best to stay on the trail. Areas of this loop will feel like a green tunnel during the warmer months and provides the perfect refuge from the hustle and bustle. At about mile 0.5, the trail will meet the banks of Eagle Creek and cut right, following the creek downstream. At about mile 1.0, the trail connects with Trail 2. Hikers may hear and see traffic from I-865 as the trail begins to curve back around to the north, moving away from the interstate. Around 1.2 miles, the trail crosses over a small tributary stream of Eagle Creek. As hikers make their way north, the trail connects briefly with Trail 4 on the westernmost part of the park before reconnecting with Trail 2 again. At about mile 1.7 the trail turns left onto Trail 3 and climbs the metal staircase leading out of the ravine and back toward the trailhead under a powerline easement. Be sure to bring bug spray for this hike as the floodplain forest and riparian area are the perfect habitat for mosquitos.

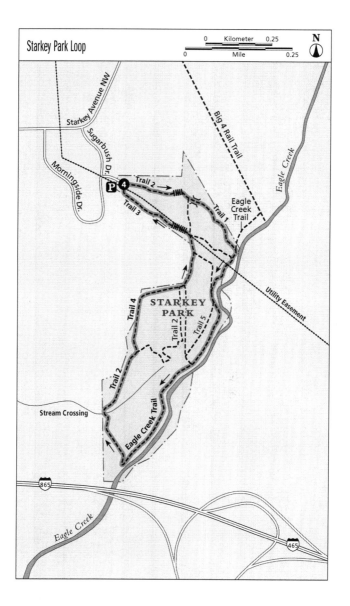

History

This 80-acre park was named after Lucile Starkey who handed down a considerable portion of the land to the town of Zionsville to be utilized as a nature park. Eagle Creek, which runs through Starkey Park, is the water source that drains into the 1,300-acre Eagle Creek Reservoir downstream.

Miles and Directions

0.0 Start from the Starkey Park parking lot, via the trailhead to the north that enters the woods, not the eastern trailhead along the powerline easement.

0.2 Continue straight past an unmarked trail junction, and then head down the steep metal stairs. At the bottom of the stairs, continue straight past the marked junction for Trail 2 and cross the bridge.

0.5 Here, the trail meets the banks of Eagle Creek and turns right onto Eagle Creek Trail 1. Continue along the creek. You will pass a trail junction for Trail 3 as you near the powerline easement.

0.6 At the large trail junction, turn left and then continue straight.

0.8 Continue straight, staying on Eagle Creek Trail 1 as you move south along Eagle Creek.

1.1 The trail curves back north and becomes Trail 2 as you approach I-865.

1.2 Cross a shallow tributary of Eagle Creek.

1.3 Turn left onto Trail 4 at the junction of Trails 2 and 4.

1.6 Turn left onto Trail 2 at the intersection of Trails 2, 4, and 5.

1.7 Turn left at the Trail 3 junction as you reach the powerline easement and climb the steep metal stairs.

2.0 Arrive at the parking lot.

5 Fort Harrison State Park: Fall Creek/Camp Creek Trails

This park is a natural sanctuary, just minutes from downtown Indianapolis, providing the perfect afternoon or weekend adventure. The trail begins nestled along Fall Creek surrounded by classic midwestern woods before climbing a series of staircases and boardwalks that offer beautiful views of the river and valley below. After passing a duck pond, the trail winds through a shaded ravine back toward the trailhead.

Distance: 2.7-mile loop
Hiking time: 1.5-2 hours
Difficulty: Moderate due to some hills and staircases
Trail surface: A mix of gravel and natural surface singletrack with a section of wooden staircases and boardwalks
Best season: Spring and fall for wildflowers and fall colors
Other trail users: Joggers
Canine compatibility: Leashed dogs permitted

Fees and permits: Entrance fee charged
Schedule: Open 7 a.m. to dusk Apr through Oct, and 8 a.m. to dusk Nov through Mar
Maps: Available at both entrance gates and at the visitor center
Trail contact: Fort Harrison State Park, 5753 Glenn Rd., Indianapolis 46216; (317) 591-0904; www.in.gov/dnr/parklake/2982 .htm

Finding the trailhead: From downtown Indianapolis, take I-70 E for 4.9 miles, then take exit 89 toward I-465 N. Continue on I-465 N for 2.5 miles, then take exit 40 and turn right onto East 56th Street, toward the city of Lawrence. After 2.1 miles, turn left onto Post Road. Follow Post Road until it terminates at East 59th Street. Turn left on East 59th Street following signs for Fort Harrison State Park. At the first intersection after the gatehouse, turn right on Clark Road toward Delaware Lake Picnic Area. GPS: N39 52.36' / W86 01.11'

The Hike

Indiana's flora and fauna surround the Fall Creek/Camp Creek loop as it guides hikers through classic midwestern creekside and woodland terrain. The trail begins at the Fall Creek Trailhead, located on the northeast corner of the Delaware Lake Picnic Area. Starting alongside Fall Creek, the trail winds through a diverse forest that includes bur oak, sycamore, and elm, just to name a few. About a mile in, the trail gains elevation via a series of staircases and boardwalks and eventually offers a beautiful view of Fall Creek. While in the higher reaches of this trail, the scenery changes to a forest of mostly oak and hickory. Along this section of the trail, be sure to keep an eye out for stone historical markers indicating old property boundaries from the park's military base era and don't forget to enjoy the view. About 1.5 miles in, the trail crosses over the paved Harrison Trace Trail and becomes the Camp Creek Trail. The trail leads past a duck pond before descending into a ravine and connecting back with the Fall Creek Trail near the trailhead. This entire area is great for birdwatching as it provides a habitat for species like the great crested flycatcher and the hooded warbler in an otherwise urban area.

History

Native Americans inhabited this region at least 8,000 years before European settlement until they were removed in the 1800s when settlers from Kentucky and Ohio expanded into this area and established homesteads. An agricultural

Fort Harrison State Park: Fall Creek/Camp Creek Trails

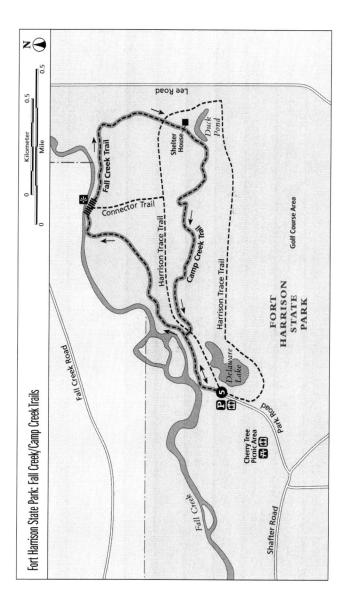

economy overtook the region leading to clear-cutting forests for crops. The creation of a military post came about due to wartime needs. In 1906, the fort was named Fort Benjamin Harrison in honor of the twenty-third president of the United States. In 1995, a portion of the park was given to the Indiana Department of Natural Resources to be used as a state park.

On March 22, 1824, the Fall Creek Massacre took place about 30 miles upstream from today's Fort Harrison State Park. Five white men murdered nine Native American men, women, and children along Fall Creek for no known reason. Four of the men were caught while one escaped. Three were convicted of murder and hanged on the banks of Fall Creek. One man, an 18-year-old, was convicted but later pardoned because of his age.

Miles and Directions

0.0 Begin from the trailhead within the Delaware Lake Picnic Area and follow Fall Creek trail markers.

0.2 Continue straight past the marked intersection with the Camp Creek Trail.

0.8 Continue straight after the boardwalk, where an unnamed connector trail Ts into Fall Creek Trail. (**Option**: Take a right onto the unnamed connector trail to connect with the paved Harrison Trace Trail and cut the hiking distance in half.)

1.3 Cross over the paved Harrison Trace Trail and continue onto Camp Creek Trail.

1.5 Turn right following signs for the Camp Creek Trail.

2.4 Turn left onto the paved Harrison Trace Trail and continue for about 40 yards until the marked turnoff to the right that reconnects with Fall Creek Trail moving toward the trailhead.

2.7 Arrive back at the trailhead.

Day Trips: Trails within an Hour of Indianapolis

6 Strawtown Koteewi Park: Northern and Southern Trail Loops

This trail leads hikers through a natural prairie along the White River rich with human history. The 750-acre park protects 142 archaeological sites, including a village the size of a football field that was constructed by the first peoples to call the land we know as Indiana home. Be sure to visit the Taylor Center of Natural History to learn about the land's history.

Distance: 5.8-mile loop
Hiking time: 2.5–3.5 hours
Difficulty: Moderate due to length of trail
Trail surface: Crushed gravel
Best season: Year-round, fall colors
Other trail users: Equestrians, bikers, joggers
Canine compatibility: Leashed dogs permitted
Fees and permits: None

Schedule: Daily, dawn to dusk
Maps: Available at the Taylor Center of Natural History
Trail contacts: Hamilton County Parks and Recreation, 12308 Strawtown Ave., Noblesville 46060; (317) 770-4400. Strawtown Koteewi Park and Taylor Nature Center; (317) 774-2574; https://www.hamiltoncounty.in .gov/Facilities/Facility/Details/ Strawtown-Koteewi-Park-11

Finding the trailhead: From downtown Indianapolis, navigate to I-65 S from North Delaware Street. In 0.4 mile keep left and take exit 112A for I-70 E. In 3.3 miles, take exit 89 and follow signs for I-465 N. In 6.9 miles, take exit 37 for I-69 N / IN 37 N toward Fort Wayne. In 3.4 miles take exit 205 for IN 37 N toward Noblesville. In 13 miles, follow Strawtown Avenue and signs for Strawtown Koteewi Park to your destination. GPS: N40 07.54' / W85 57.02'

The Hike

What this park lacks in striking views and terrain, it makes up for in natural history and cultural education. Strawtown Koteewi Park leads hikers through riparian areas, dense forests, vast prairies, and wetlands, and can—at times—feel tedious, especially while in the prairie of the southern loop where sun exposure and wind are more intense. A visit to the Taylor Center of Natural History before hiking will provide some context for the wide-open expanses of this trail. The hike begins in the north end of the parking area of the Taylor Center of Natural History where it moves toward the White River. Shortly after, hikers will pass the canoe launch and parallel the river, enjoying the hardwood forest and calm water. At about mile 0.6, the trail passes a spur on the right as it moves away from the river for a short time. After about 1.3 miles hikers will stay right and cross under a bridge to connect to the Southern Trail Loop. In this section of the trail, hikers have the option to rest with a view of the White River, various wetlands, and prairies on the several bench swings along the route. Various trail junctions may make you second guess your route on this loop, but when in doubt, stay on the path that looks most traveled. After 4.7 miles, the trail reconnects to the Northern Trail Loop to complete the loop.

History

Koteewi (pronounced ko-TAY-way) is the Miami word for "fire." Historians aren't sure whether the prairie that was once here—and is now being brought back—developed naturally as a result of flooding, or whether it developed after native peoples cleared the ground. At any rate, this area of the White River was subject to regular flooding before modern farmers built a levee on the east side of the park. The floods of this area brought nutrients to the soil, creating excellent farming opportunities that have caught the attention of various peoples throughout history. Due to westward European expansion, Strawtown served as a home to the Miami and then the Delaware tribes, as native peoples were being removed and pushed west from their homelands. So far, 142 archaeological sites have been identified, unearthing rare items that can be seen at the Taylor Center of Natural History.

Miles and Directions

0.0   Begin in the Taylor Center of Natural History parking lot at the Northern Trail Loop trailhead, near a hitching post for horses.

0.1   The trail intersects with the concrete path to the canoe launch. Follow the gravel trail to the left.

0.2   Take a right at the large three-way intersection when you enter the forest.

0.6   Follow the gravel trail to the left, avoiding the dirt path that dead ends shortly after it enters the woods.

1.3   Turn right, moving into the forest and toward the river. (**Option**: Turn left and another left at the horse trailer parking lot. This will cut out the Southern Trail Loop, shortening the trail to about 2.3 miles.)

1.5   As the trail nears Strawtown Avenue continue on the trail toward the riverbank and cross under the bridge.

1.7   Turn right as the trail meets a T junction. This signifies the start of the Southern Trail Loop.

2.2   Continue straight past the junction.

2.5   Continue straight on the main trail as you pass the fourth bench swing and a trail junction.

Strawtown Koteewi Park

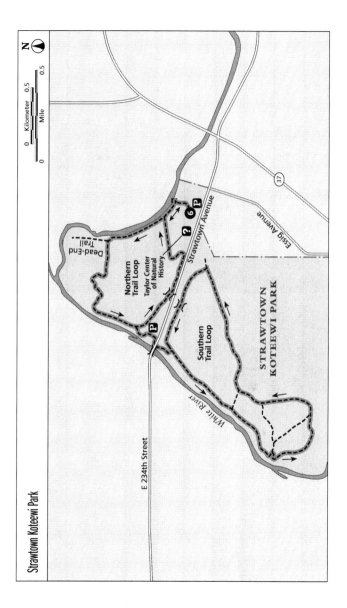

2.9 Stay straight at the fifth bench swing, past the trail junction to the left.

3.3 Continue straight past the trail junction.

3.4 Continue straight past the trail junction.

4.1 As the trail approaches the northern end of the Southern Trail Loop, follow the gravel trail left as it parallels Strawtown Avenue.

4.5 Take a right toward the forest and cross under the bridge from mile 1.5, following the path you traveled earlier.

4.7 After passing under the bridge, continue back down the previously traveled path.

4.9 As the trail Ts into the Northern Trail Loop, take a right, reentering the field.

5.7 Continue straight past the three-way intersection and past the canoe launch, toward the trailhead.

5.8 Arrive back at the trailhead.

7 McCloud Nature Park Loop

The 232 acres of McCloud Nature Park boast 6.5 miles of well-marked trails along Big Walnut Creek. This 3.4-mile loop and lollipop trail presents a variety of Indiana ecosystems including multiple successional areas, mature woodlands, and floodplain forest as you wind around its mellow hills.

Distance: 3.4-mile loop and lollipop

Hiking time: 2–2.5 hours

Difficulty: Moderate due to some hilly terrain

Trail surface: Natural surface, gravel, and grass

Best season: Summer and fall for creek crossings and fall colors

Other trail users: None

Canine compatibility: Leashed dogs permitted

Fees and permits: None

Schedule: Open daily from dawn to dusk, year-round

Maps: Available at the Nature Center

Trail contacts: Hendricks County Parks and Recreation, 955 E Main St., PO Box 463, Danville 46122; (317) 718-6188. McCloud Nature Center, 8518 Hughes Rd., North Salem 46165; (765) 676-5437; https://hendrickscountyparks.org/our-parks/mccloud-nature-park/

Finding the trailhead: From Indianapolis take US 36 W for about 23 miles. After passing through New Winchester, turn right at Putnam CR 900 E and continue for 4.5 miles before turning right onto Hughes Road. McCloud Nature Park will be on the left. You'll find the trailhead in a small gravel lot just before the Nature Center. GPS: N39 49.99' / W86 40.73'

The Hike

McCloud Nature Park is bisected by Big Walnut Creek and is connected by a single iron bridge at the southwestern corner of the property. The trails along the southern banks of the river host floodplain forests and a wide prairie, while the northern trails provide a tall forested ridge adorned with a hilltop meadow. This 3.4-mile trail begins on a mowed path within the tall grasses of Paw Paw Pathway. Once at Acorn Pass, the trail turns right. Around mile 0.4 hikers descend out of a pristine woodland area and into a successional field as the path nears Sycamore Bend Trail. Following Big Walnut Creek downstream, hikers will follow the mowed path through the tall grasses. In early spring these areas are filled with stunning ephemeral wildflowers; these flowers bloom early and are short lived. Around mile 0.8 the trail turns right where it crosses a parking area to the floodplain forest on the other side, following the river as it bends south. Shortly after, the trail connects to the Red-Tailed Ridge Trail, and follows it to Big Walnut Crossing Trail where it crosses the 1913 iron bridge over Big Walnut Creek. Continue on the western side of the riverbank toward Coyote Ridge, enjoying the scenic overlooks along the way. Around mile 1.7 the trail turns right for Woodland Way and shortly after takes a second right down the gravel road for the Whitetail Ravine loop. At the end of the Whitetail Ravine loop, the trail follows the previous path back to the iron bridge. After crossing back over the bridge, hikers will follow the signs for the Big Walnut Crossing Trail which will lead to the Nature Center. From there, hikers can follow the park road back to the parking area and trailhead.

History

In 2002 the Hendricks County Parks and Recreation Department opened the McCloud Nature Park. This, along with Solidas Nature Park, was opened in an effort to expand the county's outdoor recreation areas.

Miles and Directions

0.0 Start from the parking lot on the north side of the park road, before you reach the Nature Center. Follow Paw Paw Pathway downhill, marked on trail markers with two downward-facing pawpaw leaves. After 240 feet, you'll reach the Paw Paw Pathway loop. Turn right onto the Paw Paw Pathway toward the grassy trail.

0.1 After a bend, turn right onto Acorn Pass, identified on trail directional signs with an acorn.

0.4 A little farther ahead, just out of the woods, take a right where Acorn Pass Ts at Sycamore Bend Trail.

0.8 Turn right across the bridge.

0.9 Cross the parking lot at the end of the park road. Continue on the trail as it reenters the forest along Big Walnut Creek.

1.1 Merge onto the gravel road and continue uphill toward the iron bridge.

1.2 Turn right onto the Big Walnut Crossing Trail, identified on trail directional markers with a bridge over a river, crossing the iron bridge over Big Walnut Creek.

1.5 Turn right onto Coyote Ridge, identified on trail directional markers with two paw prints. In 600 feet, continue straight past the overlook turnoff.

1.7 Turn right for Woodland Way, identified on trail directional markers with a single leaf.

1.8 Turn right down the hill onto the gravel path for the Whitetail Ravine, identified on trail directional markers with antlers.

1.9 At the bottom of the valley, turn right taking a counter-clockwise path around the Whitetail Ravine loop. (**Caution**: This area is prone to flooding after rains; proper footwear is needed.)

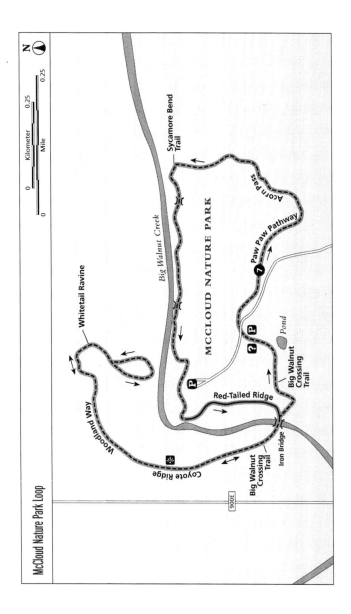

McCloud Nature Park Loop

McCLOUD NATURE PARK

Whitetail Ravine

Woodland Way

Coyote Ridge

Red-Tailed Ridge

Big Walnut Crossing Trail

Big Walnut Crossing Trail

Iron Bridge

Big Walnut Creek

Sycamore Bend Trail

Acorn Pass

Paw Paw Pathway

Pond

900E

N

Kilometer   0.25

0   Mile   0.25

2.3 Turn right at the end of Whitetail Ravine loop, following your previously traveled path toward the iron bridge.

3.0 After you cross the iron bridge, continue straight on the Big Walnut Crossing Trail moving toward the Nature Center, and soon thereafter take a left, following signs for the Nature Center, identified on trail directional markers as a house.

3.2 At the pond, turn left toward the Nature Center, and wrap around the eastern side of the building. Once you pass the Nature Center, follow the gravel road back to the parking lot.

3.4 Arrive back at the trailhead.

8 Mounds State Park: Trail 5

Mounds State Park combines serene riverside trails, unique human and natural history, and wildlife viewing areas for a wonderfully well-rounded outdoor experience. Trail 5 loops casually through hardwood forests as it parallels the White River and leads hikers past multiple historical and archaeological sites, including the Great Mound—the largest existing Native American earthwork within Indiana.

Distance: 2.5-mile loop
Hiking time: 1–1.5 hours
Difficulty: Moderate due to hilly terrain
Trail surface: Natural surface with some gravel areas
Best season: Fall for changing leaves and winter just after fresh snowfall
Other trail users: Joggers
Canine compatibility: Leashed dogs permitted

Fees and permits: Entrance fee charged
Schedule: 7 a.m. to 11 p.m., year-round
Maps: Available at entrance gates and Nature Center
Trail contact: Mounds State Park, 4306 Mounds Rd., Anderson 46017; (765) 642-6627; https://www.in.gov/dnr/parklake/2977.htm

Finding the trailhead: From Indianapolis, take I-70 E for 4.9 miles. Take exit 89 for I-465 N. Continue on I-465 N until you reach exit 37 for I-69 N toward Fort Wayne. After about 25 miles, take exit 226 for IN 9 N / IN 109 S toward Anderson. Shortly after, turn left onto Scatterfield Road and continue for 2.7 miles before turning right onto eastbound IN 232 / Mounds Road. After 1.5 miles turn left to stay on Mounds Road. After 0.5 mile the park entrance will be on the left. GPS: N40 5.75' / W85 37.15'

The Hike

Trail 5 begins at the main entrance gate of the park and loops around the outer park boundary. Shortly after beginning, the trail passes the two-story, brick Bronnenburg homestead on the right. As it continues down Trail 5, hikers have the opportunity to connect with Trail 1 for a very short detour to the Great Mound. This Native American earthwork is the largest of its kind within Mounds State Park, as well as the state of Indiana. Continuing on Trail 5, hikers will reach the White River as the trail loops north and heads upstream. Keep a lookout for wildlife in this section. Waterfowl, songbirds, whitetail deer, and other fauna frequent the river and its tributaries. As the trail loops east, it moves away from the river and into the gentle hills of the surrounding hardwood forest. Trail 5 will eventually turn south, leading back to the main entrance area. This trail is perfect for all seasons but is particularly beautiful during the spring wildflower bloom, the fall color change, and after a light snowfall.

History

Archaeological studies have derived that ancient Native Americans settled in this area as far back as 10,000 years ago. However, the most significant alterations to the landscape didn't take place until around 2,000 years ago by the Adena and Hopewell peoples. These cultures built ten earthworks in what is now Mounds State Park over a period of time spanning 300 years. Native Americans built more than 300 earthworks in east-central Indiana and thousands more throughout the Ohio Valley. The earthworks at Mounds State Park are unique due to their well-preserved state, largely due to the park's protection. Historians do not know what the mound builders called themselves 2,000 years ago but have decided to call them the Adena and Hopewell cultures based on two archaeological sites in Ohio. The Adena people are believed to be the earlier culture, living in southern Ohio and parts of Indiana, Kentucky, and West Virginia. The Hopewell people came afterward, living in Ohio, Indiana, and Illinois. Evidence at Mounds State Park suggests that both cultures lived here at different times.

Miles and Directions

0.0 Start from the trailhead near the Bronnenburg home, heading west.

0.2 Continue straight as the trail splits at the education kiosk, moving away from the unmarked Trail 1. (**Note**: If you turn right onto Trail 1 at this junction, about 80 yards in is the Great Mound, which is worth a visit. Return to Trail 5 from the way you came.)

0.3 Continue straight on Trail 5 passing the second unmarked Trail 1 juncture.

0.4 Continue straight on Trail 5 passing the third unmarked Trail 1 juncture.

0.7 Continue straight on Trail 5 passing the Trail 1 juncture on the right, continuing along the banks of the White River.

0.9 Where the trail forks at the unmarked Trail 2 junction in the river bottom, stay left on Trail 5.

1.2 Continue straight on Trail 5 past the first right-hand junction for Trail 3. (**Option**: Take a right here to visit the park's fen, a biologically sensitive wetlands area.) Just a few yards after the first junction with Trail 3, cross over a small wooden bridge and come to the second junction with Trail 3. Stay to the left and head uphill on Trail 5.

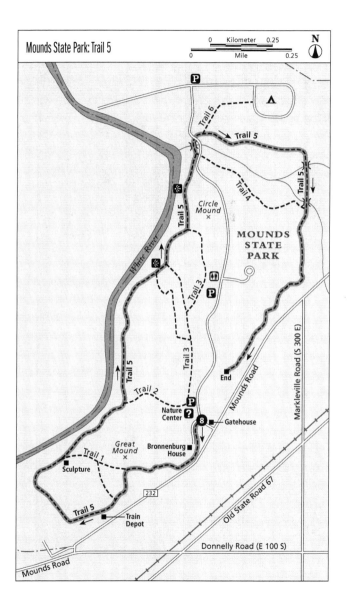

Mounds State Park: Trail 5

0   Kilometer   0.25
0   Mile   0.25

N

Trail 6

Trail 5

Trail 5

Trail 4

Circle
Mound ×

MOUNDS
STATE
PARK

Trail 5

Trail 3

Trail 3

P

White River

Trail 5

Trail 3

End

Mounds Road

Markleville Road (S 300 E)

Trail 2

P

Nature
Center

?

8   Gatehouse

Great
Mound ×

Bronnenburg
House

Trail 1

Sculpture

232

Trail 5

Train
Depot

Old State Road 67

Donnelly Road (E 100 S)

Mounds Road

1.4 At a four-way junction with Trail 3 again, you'll see the Woodland Shelter straight ahead. Stay left to continue on Trail 5 around the curve.

1.6 Cross the park road and continue into the woods on Trail 5 to the unmarked T junction. Then turn left (downhill), paralleling the park road and crossing the stream to the junction with Trail 6. Follow the sign for Trail 5 and take a right, heading east, away from the river.

1.9 Continue straight on Trail 5 past the marked Trail 4, and shortly after turn right at the unmarked T junction for Trail 5, moving around the outermost part of the park.

2.1 Keep left at another junction with Trail 4, this one unmarked. Follow Trail 5 around the park's perimeter for the next 0.4 mile until you reach the end at the gatehouse.

2.5 Arrive at the entrance gate at the end of the trail.

9 Westwood Park: Mountain Biking/ Hiking Trail

This nearly 10-mile perimeter trail surrounding Westwood Lake offers one of the longer excursions near Indianapolis—and it's well worth the distance. The clockwise loop around the reservoir provides intermittent scenic lake views, wildlife viewing opportunities, shaded respite from the summer sun, and a great workout.

Distance: 9.3-mile loop
Hiking time: 4–5 hours
Difficulty: More challenging due to length of trail
Trail surface: Natural surface singletrack
Best season: Late fall for changing leaves and wildlife sightings
Other trail users: Mountain bikers, equestrians, joggers
Canine compatibility: Leashed dogs permitted

Fees and permits: Entry fee charged
Schedule: Open daily from dawn to dusk, year-round
Maps: Available at entrance gate
Trail contact: Big Blue River Conservancy District, 1900 S Henry CR 275 W, New Castle 47362; (765) 987-1232; https://visit westwood.com

Finding the trailhead: From Indianapolis take I-70 W for 32 miles. Take exit 123 for IN 3 N toward New Castle. Continue on IN 3 N for 6 miles, then turn left onto IN 38. Continue for 2 miles, watching for signs for Westwood Recreation Area. Turn left onto Westwood Road/ Greensboro Pike and continue for 1 mile. Turn right onto Henry CR 100 S until you reach a T junction at Henry CR 275 W. Turn left and continue for 0.75 mile before turning left into Westwood Park. Take the second left after the gatehouse into the gravel parking area. GPS: N39 53.96' / W85 26.25'

The Hike

Westwood Park hosts two trails that circumnavigate the Westwood Park Reservoir: the horse trail and the shared hiking and mountain biking trail. The horse trail and the shared use trail occasionally overlap in well-marked areas. For the safety of park visitors, it's asked that hikers move clockwise around the loop while mountain bikers ride counterclockwise. The rolling foothills that surround Westwood Lake offer a more rugged experience than many trails of the surrounding area. Hikers will experience exposed roots and a few small switchbacks along the trail—features for which you usually have to travel to southern Indiana. The loop begins on the north end of the gravel parking area. While circling the reservoir, you'll experience many gradual descents and ascents into and out of ravine bottoms all while surrounded by a thick forest. A grove of tall pines and two meadows break up the scenery, providing some diversity. At the southern end of the loop you'll pass through the spillway of the reservoir's dam, which offers quite the view. Westwood Park is a haven for Indiana wildlife. Whitetail deer, colorful mallards, speedy chipmunks, and various bird species are common sights while on the trail. If you're lucky, you may get to see a bald eagle dive for a fish. Be mindful of the length of this trail. Nearly 10 miles is a long day for anyone: Be prepared with plenty of water, snacks, and proper hiking equipment, and be aware that there are no alternate trails to cut this length short, as it covers the perimeter of the reservoir.

History

Westwood Park was developed by the Big Blue River Conservancy District (BBRCD) and opened to the public in 1974. The BBRCD was established in 1965 under the Indiana Conservancy Act in order to solve water management issues within Henry and Rush Counties. The park's 180-acre reservoir, formed by an earthen dam, is fed by Westwood Run which is a tributary of the Big Blue River. This reservoir serves as sediment storage and flood control for the Big Blue River and provides municipal and industrial water supplies to the surrounding area.

Miles and Directions

0.0 Start from the trailhead near the wooden changing stations in the gravel parking lot. You'll head to the right of the trailhead sign to start the trail. (**Note**: Hikers must travel clockwise around the loop.)

0.2 Continue straight at the first trail junction and cross the first bridge. Once crossing over the second bridge, follow the left fork of the trail. (**Note**: There are many small bridges on this trail and they can be very slippery when wet.)

0.3 Continue straight over the horse trail and cross the paved park road to the trail on the other side. The DO NOT ENTER trail markers apply only to horse and mountain bike traffic.

3.3 Cross over the bridge at the northern end of the lake.

5.2 Cross over the horse trail and continue straight back into the woods. Be sure to yield to horse traffic here.

5.4 Cross over the horse trail and continue straight again, through the split rail fence. Be sure to yield to horse traffic.

7.7 Hiker and horse traffic merge. Be aware of other trail users.

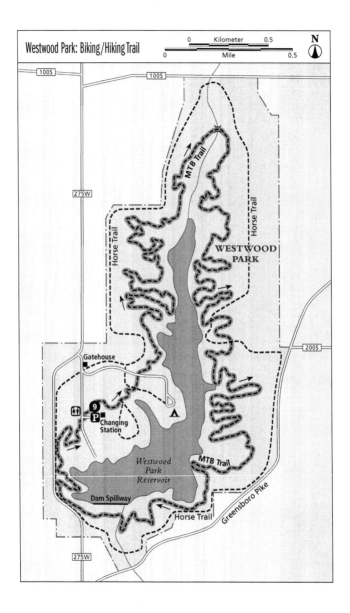

Westwood Park: Biking/Hiking Trail

N

Kilometer
0   0.5
Mile
0   0.5

100S   100S

275W

Horse Trail

MTB Trail

WESTWOOD
PARK

Horse Trail

200S

Gatehouse

9
P
Changing
Station

Westwood
Park
Reservoir

MTB Trail

Dam Spillway

Horse Trail

Greensboro Pike

275W

7.8 Shared use section of the trail ends as you continue through the split rail fence, following the trail that is closest to the lakeshore. Continue following the trail back toward the parking lot.

8.1 Cross the spillway.

8.3 Continue past the dam.

9.3 Arrive back at the trailhead.

10 Morgan-Monroe State Forest: Low Gap Trail

The Low Gap Trail in Morgan–Monroe State Forest is perfect for the hiker looking to extend their endurance. At just over 10 miles, it's one of the longest continuous trails in the area. Those willing to brave the distance will be rewarded with serene forests, unique overhanging rock walls, and a great workout.

Distance: 10.2-mile loop
Hiking time: 4–5 hours
Difficulty: More challenging due to hilly terrain and distance
Trail surface: Natural surfaces and some gravel fire/service roads
Best season: Spring and fall for wildflowers and fall colors
Other trail users: None
Canine compatibility: Leashed dogs permitted

Fees and permits: None
Schedule: Open 24 hours, year-round
Maps: Located in the Morgan-Monroe State Forest brochure
Trail contact: Morgan-Monroe State Forest, 6220 Forest Rd., Martinsville 46151; (765) 342- 4026; https://www.hoosierhikerscouncil.org/morgan-monroe-forest

Finding the trailhead: From Indianapolis take IN 37 S and continue for 27 miles toward Martinsville. Take exit 134 toward Liberty Church Road and continue for 0.4 mile. Turn left onto Godsey Road and continue for 0.3 mile before turning right onto East Hacker Creek Road/Old State Road 37 S. Continue on Old State Road 37 S for 4.1 miles and then turn left onto Main Forest Road. Continue for 3.1 miles. The trailhead will be on your right and shares a trailhead with the Rock Shelter Trail. GPS: N39 18.66' / W86 25.49'

The Hike

The 24,000-acre state forest hosts 27 miles of hiking trails within its rich forest. The 10.2-mile Low Gap Trail mostly follows a singletrack trail, but does connect with a few service roads. The trail begins in a gravel parking area on Forest Road. Moving west, the trail parallels Forest Road briefly before turning left onto the gravel path, Tincher Ridge. The trail follows this service road for about a mile before turning left onto the singletrack trail. Moving down the ridge, hikers enter Sweedy Hollow Nature Preserve via a series of switchbacks. This hollow is a unique section of the loop, offering a dramatically steep landscape of overhanging cliffs and large boulders. The botany enthusiast will enjoy this section due to its rare plant species, including Guyandotte beauty and small whorled pogonia. Around mile 1.6 the trail reaches the Rock Shelter—a large overhanging rock feature that the trail passes under. This marks the series of switchbacks leading to the ridge above. At mile 2.4 the trail turns right to continue on the Low Gap Trail. About 1.5 miles later, hikers will cross over Low Gap Trail Road and enter the 2,700-acre backcountry area. This area provides protection for many endangered species such as the Indiana bat and timber rattlesnake. From here the trail ascends to Gorley Ridge, where it continues for about half a mile before descending into another hollow and once again ascending to the next ridge. Around mile 6.0 the trail follows Orcutt Road, leading to the second crossing of Low Gap Road. Orcutt Road becomes East Tulip Tree Trace Road here. Follow the road, passing a few private properties and a radio tower. Around mile 8.8 the trail reconnects with a signed singletrack that parallels Forest Road. At mile 9.9, hikers can turn left onto the gravel road to visit the 130-year-old Draper Cabin. Turn left once you've traveled back up the gravel road from the cabin to continue toward the trailhead.

History

In the late 1800s settlers clear-cut what is now Morgan-Monroe State Forest to make room for agricultural needs. Over-farming resulted in depleted soil by the early 1900s. Between 1929 and 1930 the first land acquisitions and restoration efforts were made for the soon-to-become state forest. With time and continued restoration efforts, the forest regained its integrity and has provided important research for forestry management.

Miles and Directions

0.0 Start from the trailhead located along Forest Road and head west onto Low Gap, Rock Shelter, and Tecumseh Trails. Be sure to sign the trail register. For the next few hundred feet, continue to follow the white diamond blazes painted on trees, as you cross a paved path and head toward Tincher Ridge. (**Note**: Throughout this trail, always look for and follow white diamond blazes painted on trees.)

0.1 Take a left down the gravel service road (Tincher Ridge).

0.7 Turn left onto the singletrack Low Gap Trail that leads downhill toward Sweedy Hollow Nature Preserve, following the brown trail marker for the Tecumseh Trail.

1.0 Turn left to stay on Low Gap Trail, following the brown trail marker for the Tecumseh Trail and the diamond and rectangle white trail blazes.

1.6 Pass Rock Shelter on the right.

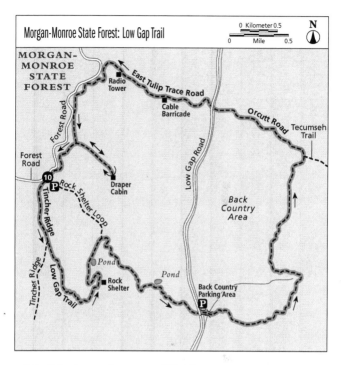

Morgan-Monroe State Forest: Low Gap Trail

0 Kilometer 0.5
0 Mile 0.5

N

MORGAN-
MONROE
STATE
FOREST

East Tulip Trace Road

Radio
Tower

Cable
Barricade

Orcutt Road

Tecumseh
Trail

Forest Road

Forest
Road

10 P

Rock Shelter Loop

Draper
Cabin

Low Gap Road

Tincher Ridge

Low Gap Trail

Pond

Rock
Shelter

Pond

Back
Country
Area

Back Country
Parking Area

P

1.7 Take the wooden steps uphill, following the brown trail marker for Tecumseh Trail, and white diamond blazes painted on trees.

2.4 After a slight uphill, you'll reach a marked trail junction connecting the Rock Shelter Loop. Turn right to stay on Low Gap Trail toward the backcountry area. (**Option**: Turn left here to return to the trailhead, shortening the tail to about 3 miles.)

4.0 Cross Low Gap Road and pass over two footbridges passing the backcountry parking area on the left. You are now in the backcountry area of this loop.

6.7 Turn left to stay on the Low Gap Trail at the sign marking the Tecumseh Trail junction. The trail travels along the gravel Orcutt Road.

7.8 Cross Low Gap Road again, now heading up the gravel East Tulip Tree Trace Road on the other side. Continue west on East Tulip Tree Trace Road.

8.3 East Tulip Tree Trace Road ends at a cable barricade. Continue past the barricade, where the road becomes a service road again.

8.8 Shortly after passing the radio tower, turn left off the road and onto the signed singletrack trail, following signs for the Low Gap Trail.

9.9 Continue straight across the gravel road. (**Option**: Turn left down the gravel road to reach Draper Cabin, retracing your steps back to this point when you're done, adding about 1 mile to the hike.)

10.2 Arrive back at the trailhead.

Worth a Drive: Trails over an Hour from Indianapolis

11 Beanblossom Bottoms Nature Preserve

The wetlands of Beanblossom Bottoms Nature Preserve are a nice change of pace from the rolling hills of southern Indiana. This 3.4-mile loop takes place mostly on a flat boardwalk, guiding hikers through wooded swamps, successional fields, and marshland. This preserve provides a unique experience of a biologically diverse ecosystem within Indiana.

Distance: 3.4-mile loop
Hiking time: 1.5–2 hours
Difficulty: Easy due to flat terrain
Trail surface: Boardwalk, some natural surface
Best season: Late spring for flower blooms
Other trail users: None
Canine compatibility: Leashed dogs permitted •
Fees and permits: None
Schedule: Open daily from dawn to dusk

Maps: Available online at www.in .gov/dnr/naturepreserve
Trail contacts: Sycamore Land Trust, PO Box 7801, Bloomington 47407; (812) 336-5382. The Indiana Department of Natural Resources, Division of Nature Preserves, 402 W Washington St., Room W267, Indianapolis 46204; (317) 232-4052; www.in .gov/dnr/naturepreserve

Finding the trailhead: From Indianapolis, take IN 37 S toward Martinsville. After Martinsville, IN 37 S becomes I-69 S. Continue for 10.3 miles before taking exit 125 for Sample Road. At the traffic circle, take the first exit onto Sample Road and continue for 0.6 mile. Turn left onto West Simpson Chapel Road and continue for 1.2 miles before turning right onto North Bottom Road. Continue for 2 miles until you reach the gravel North Woodall Road and turn left. After 1.2

miles, the parking area and trailhead will be on your left. GPS: N39 16.62' / W86 34.70'

The Hike

The 336.82-acre preserve is a floodplain forest bordered by successional fields and wetlands. This loop begins on a gravel path leading away from the gravel parking area and into a forest. The trail passes a meadow on the right and meets a boardwalk at mile 0.3. Moving through a meadow, which may have standing water depending on the season, the trail offers a wide view of the surrounding landscape. Around mile 0.7, the meadow will give way to a bottomland hardwood forest of swamp cottonwood, silver maple, and sycamore, among others. A bottomland hardwood forest is a mix of hardwood trees within lowland floodplains located near large waterways. This ecosystem is rare today, as the majority have been drained for agriculture, due to their rich soil contents. At mile 1.2 the trail turns right as the boardwalk splits. Shortly after, the boardwalk becomes a grass path surrounded by marshy grasslands. At mile 1.5 at the cable barricade, the trail returns toward the boardwalk. Soon, the boardwalk will rise about 3 feet from the ground as it enters a woodland swamp. The swamp's ecosystem is particularly interesting. Be sure to read the educational signs at the Swamp Observation Deck for a better understanding of how the swamp came to be. At mile 2.7 the trail reconnects to the first gravel path and takes a slight right—look for the mown path. Shortly after is the Eagle Observation Deck where hikers can scan the trees for the bald eagles' nest. Once finished, the trail returns the way it came toward the trailhead. Be aware that spring flooding can make this area impassable.

History

This preserve is owned by the Sycamore Land Trust who acquired it in 1995. This land is protected by the Wetland Reserve Program in an effort to enhance wetland areas that are retired from agricultural use. The Beanblossom area was actually drained for farming in the late nineteenth and early twentieth centuries. Once farming left this area, the natural ecosystem began to return on its own. The National Audubon Society has accredited this area, as it provides

Beanblossom Bottoms Nature Preserve

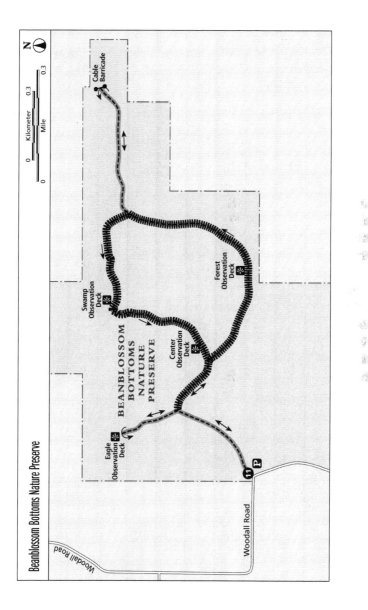

habitat for great blue herons, Wilson's snipes, barred owls, and several more bird species. It also provides a home for the state-endangered Kirtland's snake, and the unique northern crawfish frog, also known as the Hoosier frog.

Miles and Directions

0.0   Start from the trailhead at North Woodall Road.

0.3   Turn right onto the boardwalk.

0.4   Turn right at the trail junction onto the wooden bridge to take a counterclockwise tour around the boardwalk loop.

1.1   As the boardwalk splits, turn right at the fork. Continue toward the field where the trail becomes a mown grass path.

1.5   At the end of the grass path, marked by a cable barricade, turn back the way you came, toward the boardwalk.

1.8   When you reach the boardwalk, take a right.

2.6   At the end of the loop, just past the Center Observation Deck, turn right.

2.7   When you return to the gravel path, turn right and continue 0.2 mile along the mown grass path to the Eagle Observation Deck. Return back the way you came from the observation deck, turning right at the split, heading south toward the trailhead.

3.4   Arrive back at the trailhead.

12 McCormick's Creek State Park: Trail 5

Trail 5, within Indiana's first state park, is the perfect destination for those seeking a quality hike away from the typical crowds of McCormick's Creek. Wolf Cave and the Twin Bridges are the main landmarks of this trail. Visitors can take a close look at the two features, but pay attention to park signage that stresses the importance of remaining in designated areas to protect the ecosystem and structure of the natural limestone.

Distance: 2.1-mile loop

Hiking time: 1–1.5 hours

Difficulty: Moderate due to hilly terrain

Trail surface: Gravel and packed dirt

Best season: Spring for wildflower bloom

Other trail users: None

Canine compatibility: Leashed dogs permitted

Fees and permits: Entrance fee charged

Schedule: Open daily from 7 a.m. to 11 p.m., year-round

Maps: Available at entrance gates and at the Nature Center

Trail contact: McCormick's Creek State Park, 250 McCormick's Creek Park Rd., Spencer 47460; (812) 829-2235; https://www.in.gov/dnr/parklake/2978.htm

Finding the trailhead: From Indianapolis, take I-70 W. Take exit 41 in Cloverdale and turn left onto southbound US 231. Continue for 19 miles and then turn left onto IN 46 in Spencer. Follow IN 46 for 2 miles until you reach the sign for McCormick's Creek State Park on your left. Turn left into the park and follow the signs to Wolf Cave. GPS: N39 17.73' / W86 43.43'

The Hike

Most of this hike takes place in the 214-acre Wolf Cave Nature Preserve, located in the northeastern corner of the park's boundary. Trail 5 begins in a densely forested area that is dotted with sinkholes. These features can be spotted from the trail in the form of large depressions along the forest floor. Soon, hikers will cross over a fork of Litten Branch Creek two times before reaching the limestone Wolf Cave. The small creek that hikers gracefully rock-hop over flows into Wolf Cave and is particularly noticeable when the water is up. The park, and common sense, strongly discourage hiking on the slopes around and over Wolf Cave due to erosion concerns, although the cave itself is open to hikers. After Wolf Cave, Trail 5 passes the Youth Tent Area junction and then leads downhill, toward Twin Bridges. These limestone bridges, once a chamber of Wolf Cave, are the remaining rock from a collapsed cave ceiling. After Twin Bridges, hikers will navigate multiple creek crossings as the trail ascends a dense hollow of thick trees. At 1.3 miles the trail passes a small but pleasant waterfall, about 3 feet high. Once again, the trail crosses Trail 8 and not long after reaches the park road. Turn right onto the road and enjoy the short walk back to the trailhead.

History

Legend has it, Wolf Cave derived its name when an early settler named Nance Peden was traveling home from selling goods in Spencer. While walking past the cave she was chased by a pack of wolves, but threw down her bonnet and gloves and ran home safely. Wolves, due to over hunting, disappeared from Indiana in 1908. McCormick's Creek State Park and

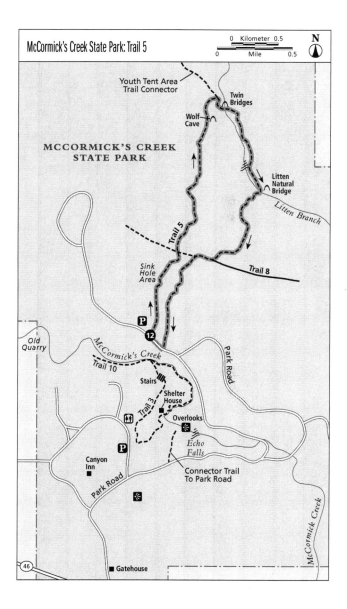

McCormick's Creek State Park: Trail 5

0   Kilometer   0.5

0   Mile   0.5

N

Youth Tent Area
Trail Connector

Twin
Bridges

Wolf
Cave

MCCORMICK'S CREEK
STATE PARK

Litten
Natural
Bridge

Litten Branch

Trail 5

Sink
Hole
Area

Trail 8

P

12

Old
Quarry

McCormick's Creek

Trail 10

Stairs

Trail 3

Shelter
House

Overlooks

Park Road

P

Canyon
Inn

Park Road

Echo
Falls

Connector Trail
To Park Road

McCormick Creek

46

Gatehouse

much of southern Indiana is dotted with limestone caves and sinkholes. These features form over time as water seeps through cracks in the limestone bedrock. Groundwater, due to it being mildly acidic, further erodes the limestone cracks into large funnel-shaped sinkholes and caverns. This type of topography, where bedrock is dissolved by groundwater to create caves and sinkholes, is known as a karst landscape. In 2009, Wolf Cave and all caves located on state properties were closed to the public by the Indiana Department of Natural Resources in hopes of reducing the spread of white-nose syndrome, a disease that has depleted much of the Indiana bat population.

Miles and Directions

0.0 Start at the trailhead via the Wolf Cave parking area.

0.3 Continue straight on Trail 5 past the four-way trail junction connecting the paved Trail 8.

0.8 Pass Wolf Cave on the right.

0.9 Pass Twin Bridges on the left.

1.2 Pass Litten Natural Bridge on the left.

1.7 Continue straight on Trail 5 past the second four-way junction with the paved Trail 8.

2.0 When you reach the park road, turn right, following the road for 0.1 mile toward the Wolf Cave parking area.

2.1 Arrive back at the trailhead.

13 Brown County State Park: CCC Trail (Trail 2)

The historic CCC Trail is a must do within the nearly 16,000 acres of Brown County State Park. This trail, carved out by the Civilian Conservation Corps, offers a unique connection to our complicated forestry history while exploring some of Indiana's highest elevations. Several historic structures along this loop, like the North Lookout Tower, offer a walk through time, backdropped by the southern Indiana foothills.

Distance: 2.2-mile loop

Hiking time: 1–1.5 hours

Difficulty: Moderate due to hilly terrain

Trail surface: Singletrack natural surface

Best season: Late fall for changing leaves

Other trail users: None

Canine compatibility: Leashed dogs permitted

Fees and permits: Entrance fee charged

Schedule: Open daily from 7 a.m. to 11 p.m., year-round

Maps: Available at entrance gate, park office, and the Nature Center

Trail contact: Brown County State Park, 1405 IN 46 W, Nashville 47448; (812) 988-6406; https://www.in.gov/dnr/parklake/2988.htm

Finding the trailhead: From Indianapolis take I-65 S for a little over 40 miles. Take exit 68 for IN 46 toward Nashville and continue for 14.2 miles where you'll turn left into Brown County State Park via the north entrance gate. Continue straight until you come to the intersection with Lodge Road. Turn left onto Lodge Road and park in the large parking area just south of the Abe Martin Lodge. The trailhead is northeast of the Abe Martin Lodge near the Lafe Bud, Tawny Apple, and Doc Mopps cabins. GPS: N39 11.25' / W86 12.88'

The Hike

The CCC Trail (Trail 2) begins just northeast of the Abe Martin Lodge, descending downhill into a wide hollow before climbing the following ridge. Around the 1-mile mark, the trail crosses Lodge Road as it leads toward the North Lookout Tower on the left. The top level of the stone and wooden structure yields a vast treetop vista of an uninterrupted forest. As visitors look out over the rolling hills, it's easy to understand why this area earned the nickname "Little Smokies." This is quite a sight considering that much of this area was clear-cut by the early 1900s. The Civilian Conservation Corps' planting of black walnut, black locust, and various pines was an important stepping stone in this forest's recovery. Please do not deface this historic structure by carving in the wood or marking the stone. Once satisfied with the view, return to the ground level and turn left to continue on the trail. Through this section of the trail, be on the lookout for some of the park's wildlife. Spring and fall turkeys can sometimes be seen as well as whitetail deer, grey squirrels, and various bird species, including cardinals and white-breasted nuthatches. At mile 2.0 the trail passes the Lower Shelter on the left, crosses a wooden bridge, and then ascends the stone staircase, reconnecting with the trailhead shortly after.

History

Established in 1929, Brown County is the largest state park in Indiana. Much of the park's infrastructure is owed to President Franklin D. Roosevelt's efforts to recover from the Great

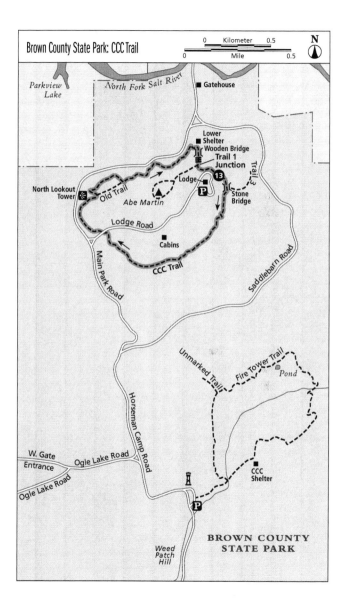

Brown County State Park: CCC Trail

Kilometer
0   0.5
Mile
0   0.5

N

Parkview Lake

North Fork Salt River

■ Gatehouse

Lower
■ Shelter
Wooden Bridge
Trail 1
Junction

Trail 3

North Lookout
Tower

Old Trail

▲
Abe Martin

■ Lodge
P
⓭
Stone
Bridge

Lodge Road

■ Cabins

CCC Trail

Main Park Road

Saddlebarn Road

Unmarked Trail

Fire Tower Trail

Pond

Horseman Camp Road

W. Gate
Entrance

Ogle Lake Road

Ogle Lake Road

P

■ CCC
Shelter

Weed
Patch
Hill

**BROWN COUNTY
STATE PARK**

Depression. The series of public works programs, known as the New Deal, prompted the creation of the Civilian Conservation Corps in 1933. The CCC built Trail 2 and all of its impressive features such as the stone bridges, staircases, the Lower Shelter, and North Lookout Tower. The North Lookout Tower, as well as the park's other towers, were used to watch for wildfires. During this time period, it was believed that the immediate extinguishing of fires was best practice. Now it's known that natural wildfires play an important role for a healthy ecosystem, providing a rejuvenation of soil nutrients and clearing overwhelming undergrowth. Today, natural wildfires (albeit rare within Indiana) are watched carefully to ensure public safety and controlled burns are induced in areas that need extra attention.

Miles and Directions

0.0 Start from the trailhead near the Lafe Bud, Tawny Apple, and Doc Mopps cabins. Shortly after coming downhill past the cabins, the trail Ts; turn right toward the stone bridge for Trail 2.

1.0 Cross over Lodge Road.

1.2 At the top of the hill, at the base of the North Lookout Tower, turn right to continue on Trail 2, or take a quick detour and climb the steps to North Lookout Tower to take in the view.

1.3 After coming downhill from the North Lookout Tower, turn left at the first trail junction to continue on Trail 2.

2.0 After passing the Lower Shelter, cross over the wooden bridge and climb uphill along the huge stone staircase. The end of the trail is at the top of the hill. (**Note:** If the stone staircase is closed, follow signs for the detour along Trail 3. This adds 0.2 mile to the hike.)

2.2 Arrive back at the trailhead.

14 Prophetstown State Park: Loop Trail

Located at the confluence of the Tippecanoe and Wabash Rivers, this state park is home to a significant amount of cultural history, as well as a distinct native landscape of prairies and woodlands. This loop and lollipop trail moves though Trails 2, 3, and 4 while guiding hikers through floodplain prairies, vast overlooks, and floodplain forests in Indiana's newest state park.

Distance: 6.4-mile loop and lollipop

Hiking time: 3–4 hours

Difficulty: Moderate due to hilly terrain

Trail surface: Paved, gravel, and dirt

Best season: Spring for bird-watching and wildflowers

Other trail users: Bikers

Canine compatibility: Leashed dogs permitted

Fees and permits: Entrance fee charged

Schedule: Open daily from 7 a.m. to 11 p.m., year-round

Maps: Available at gatehouse and entrance station

Trail contact: Prophetstown State Park, 4112 E State Road 225, West Lafayette 47906; (765) 567-4919; https://www.in .gov/dnr/parklake/2971.htm

Finding the trailhead: From Indianapolis take I-65 N to exit 178 / SR 43 north of Lafayette. Head south on SR 43 for a very short distance and turn left onto Burnett Road. Continue for about 0.4 mile. Turn right on 9th Street to Swisher Road. This is a hard left immediately after the veterinary office. Once on Swisher Road, cross over I-65 and find the park gatehouse. GPS: N40 30.56' / W86 48.20'

The Hike

This hike begins on Trail 2, located at the north end of the parking area. It follows a paved path for a short distance as it moves through a large floodplain prairie where multiple restoration projects are being carried out. Around 0.1 mile the trail becomes gravel as it begins the counterclockwise loop of Trail 3. Soon, the trail reaches the banks of the Wabash River and follows it upstream. Hikers will have views of the vast prairie to their left and the meandering waterway to their right. Around mile 1.4, the trail reaches the confluence of the Wabash and Tippecanoe Rivers. Moving through the mild hills of a shady floodplain forest, hikers will eventually connect with the Trail 4 lollipop. Here, the scenery trades off between floodplain forests and floodplain prairies. During spring and early summer, these floodplain prairies become a maze of tall grasses and wildflowers such as wild bergamot and white wild indigo. It's a great spot for birdwatching for species like the cedar waxwing and black-capped chickadee. However, some visitors may find these prairies to be scorched from recent fires. These prescribed burns help to rejuvenate the soil and make way for native plants to thrive. Trail 4 leads hikers to the northernmost point of the park and offers a view of Moots Creek before turning back toward the previously traveled path. Be advised that parts of Trails 3 and 4 are subject to occasional flooding and may be closed. Don't cross sections of the trail that are flooded. After about 5.3 miles, the trail reaches a large wooden bridge and continues 1.1 miles through the floodplain prairie toward the trailhead.

History

Prophetstown State Park derives its name from a Native American village located between the Tippecanoe and Wabash Rivers. This village was established in 1808 by two Shawnee brothers, Tecumseh and Tenskwatawa (The Prophet), who were forced to leave the Ohio area due to the advancement of European settlers. Tecumseh, in an effort to fight back against the continually advancing settlers, formed alliances with more than fourteen tribes throughout the region. These tribes met at Prophetstown to hear The Prophet speak. Concerned by their numbers, the governor of the Indiana Territory, William Henry Harrison, moved 1,200 troops to the area. The battle to follow resulted in the villagers fleeing to Wildcat Creek as Harrison's troops burned Prophetstown to the ground.

Miles and Directions

0.0 Start at the trailhead in the northeastern corner of the fishing area parking lot. Follow the paved switchbacks toward the observation deck, but before reaching the observation deck, turn left at the break in the metal railing to follow the wooden trail marker for Trail 2.

0.1 Turn right onto the paved path, and follow along the paved path to the Trail 3 trailhead. Just beyond this trailhead, turn right at the fork to take the Trail 3 loop counterclockwise.

0.3 Stay right at the fork, following the wooden trail marker for Trail 3.

1.3 Turn left and follow the mowed path and wooden trail marker for Trail 3.

1.4 Continue straight across the wash, following the trail marker for Trail 3. (**Caution**: This area is prone to flooding.)

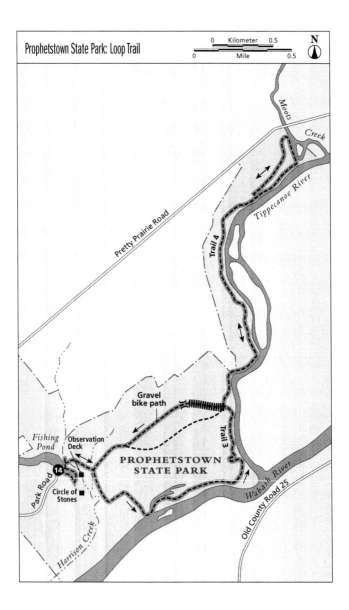

Prophetstown State Park: Loop Trail

1.8 When you reach the paved path, turn right following signs for Trails 3 and 4, along the paved path. Immediately after, continue straight along Trail 4, indicated by the wooden trail marker.

1.9 Paved path ends; continue straight on mowed path.

2.9 Keep right at the fork, following the trail markers for Trail 4.

3.1 Continue straight to cross a small creek. (**Caution**: There is no bridge here and this area is prone to flooding.) Shortly thereafter, continue straight on the mowed path moving along the river to begin the lollipop portion of Trail 4 counterclockwise.

3.9 At the T junction, turn left to rejoin Trail 4, and immediately after turn right to follow the trail back toward the trailhead.

5.1 Come out of the woods and turn left, following trail markers for Trail 3 and 4.

5.3 Continue straight onto Trail 3, and shortly thereafter turn right onto the big wooden bridge.

5.6 Once across the bridge, continue straight on the gravel trail. (**Option:** Take a sharp right turn and follow Trail 3 into the woods to finish, adding 1.1 miles.)

5.8 Keep right at the fork onto the paved path, continuing back toward the trailhead.

6.1 Keep right at the fork, following the trail marker for Trail 3.

6.2 At the T junction at the fishing pond, turn left following the paved path toward the parking lot.

6.3 Keep left, following the paved path toward the basketball courts.

6.4 Arrive back at the trailhead.

15 Shades State Park: Western Ravines Loop

When it comes to iconic hikes in Indiana, Turkey Run State Park tends to get all the love, but Shades—located just minutes away—is possibly the most overlooked hidden gem in the state. This route is packed with some of the park's best features, meandering through deep sandstone ravines, repeatedly snaking toward and away from Sugar Creek, and ending with stops along and below peaceful forest waterfalls.

Distance: 4.0-mile loop
Hiking time: 2–3 hours
Difficulty: More difficult due to length, hilly terrain, and trail surfaces
Trail surface: Natural surface singletrack, ladders, and some streambeds
Best season: Late spring for wildflower bloom
Other trail users: None
Canine compatibility: Leashed dogs permitted; not recommended due to ladder climbs
Fees and permits: Entrance fee charged
Schedule: Open daily from 7 a.m. to 11 p.m., year-round
Maps: Available at the entrance gates
Trail contact: Shades State Park, 7751 S Montgomery CR 890 W, Waveland 47989; (765) 642-6627; https://www.in.gov/dnr/parklake/2970.htm

Finding the trailhead: From Indianapolis, take I-74 W via I-465 N. Continue on I-74 W to exit 52 for IN 75 toward Jamestown. Turn left onto IN 75 S and continue for 4.3 miles. The road will bend slightly to the left and become IN 234 W. Continue on IN 234 W for 21.4 miles before turning left onto CR 800 S following signs for Shades State Park. Take the first right into the park, then continue straight until you reach Hemlock Picnic Area. The trailhead is 0.1 mile south of the parking area on the right side of the road. GPS: N39 56.12' / W87 04.60'

The Hike

Caution: *Wet weather can make the sandstone canyons and wooden ladders dangerously slick and even impassable. Before setting out, check in at the Nature Center for trail conditions and closures.*

The trail begins at the Backpack trailhead located along the road, south of the parking area. The trail will flow gently around rolling hills. Soon, the trail will weave through a grove of red pines as the gentle hills give way to steep ravines on both sides. At mile 0.75 the trail descends a wooden staircase to the creek bed path of Trail 8 where it enters Shawnee Canyon. The canyon continues for nearly half a mile before meeting Sugar Creek. The trail follows the river for a short distance before coming into Kickapoo Ravine where it meets Trail 7. At mile 1.5 the trail climbs a wooden staircase to an upland forest. Shortly after, the trail turns left onto Trail 4 and navigates rolling hills. After 2.2 miles the trail enters into Frisz Ravine. This area is uniquely narrow and blanketed with thick green moss on overhanging sandstone cliffs. The trail ascends two wooden ladders into a slot canyon where the path becomes Trail 5 and leads back toward Sugar Creek. Shortly thereafter, the trail enters Kintz Ravine for another dose of moss-covered canyons and cliffs before climbing another ladder to the Hickory Shelter House. Follow the gravel trail around the left side of the playground to connect with Trail 1. Along this section, the trail offers viewing points of the scenic Sugar Creek. At 3.4 miles the trail descends a staircase that leads to a trail spur to Silver Cascade Falls. After enjoying the scenery, head up the ravine where the trail meets Devil's Punch Bowl—a bowl-shaped canyon that has been eroded by the modest creek flowing through it. Ascend the wooden staircase and follow Trail 1 around the rim of Devil's Punch Bowl, then down a gravel path and back to the parking area.

History

Indiana's fifteenth state park came to be in 1947. In the late 1800s, the land of what is now Shades State Park was home to a forty-room inn. Joseph W. Frisz, also known as the "Father of Shades," bought the land in 1916 with the intention of expanding and protecting the property. Formerly known as "Shades of Death," the 3,082-acre state park is a favorite for outdoor recreationists.

Miles and Directions

0.0 Start from the main parking area near Hemlock Picnic Area. Hike south on the park road and turn right onto the Backpack Trail.

0.1 At the Backpack trailhead, take the right path.

0.3 Turn right at the T junction with the unnamed trail, following signs for the Backpack Trail.

0.5 Turn left to stay on the Backpack Trail at the sign that says "To Campground."

0.6 Turn right, away from the Backpack Trail and onto Trail 8, at the bottom of the ravine. Trail 8 follows the streambed; look for the trail along the sides of the trail for easiest routes. (**Note**: The sign that says "Hikers Prohibited Beyond This Point" at this junction is meant to keep hikers off canyon walls and the canyon rim. Hikers are permitted to hike in the canyon bottom.)

Shades State Park: Western Ravines Loop

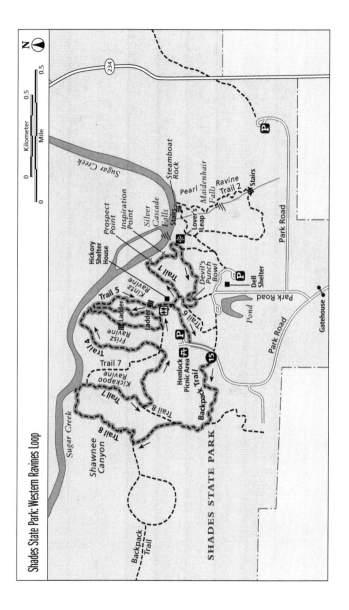

N

Kilometer 0.5

0   0.5
Mile

Sugar Creek

Steamboat Rock

Prospect Point

Inspiration Point

Silver Cascade Falls

Hickory Shelter House

Kintz Ravine

Trail 5

Ladder

Ladder

Frisz Ravine

Trail 4

Trail 7

Kickapoo Ravine

Trail 7

Trail 8

Shawnee Canyon

Trail 8

Backpack Trail

Sugar Creek

Trail 1

Trail 6

Devil's Punch Bowl

Lover's Leap

Pearl Falls

Maidenhair Falls

Ravine Trail 2

Stairs

Stairs

234

Park Road

Dell Shelter

Pond

Park Road

Park Road

Gatehouse

Hemlock Picnic Area

15

Backpack Trail

SHADES STATE PARK

1.1 Turn to the right, away from Sugar Creek, and up Kickapoo Ravine. Continue straight past the stairs on the left as Trail 8 becomes Trail 7 in Kickapoo Ravine.

1.5 Climb the stairs up out of Kickapoo Ravine and follow Trail 7 to the left.

1.7 Where the trail loop merges into itself, turn right and follow wooden trail markers for Trail 4. Turn left onto Trail 4.

2.2 Turn right, away from Sugar Creek and up Frisz Ravine at the "Trail 4 Rugged" sign.

2.5 Turn left onto Trail 5, following it back down toward Sugar Creek, and then up Kintz Ravine.

3.2 At the Hickory Shelter House, follow Trail 1 up to the left, around the left side of the playground, following the wooden trail marker for Prospect Point and Inspiration Point.

3.4 After Prospect Point and Inspiration Point, turn left to descend the staircase into the ravine. At the bottom of the staircase, turn left on a Trail 1 spur to Silver Cascade Falls. Retrace your steps to the base of the staircase and continue straight up the ravine toward Devil's Punch Bowl.

3.7 Climb the stairs out of Devil's Punch Bowl and follow the wooden trail marker for Trail 1. Follow the stairs and wooden bridge around the rim of Devil's Punch Bowl.

3.8 Turn right onto the wooden stairs at the junction with Trail 6, continuing on Trail 1.

3.9 At the T junction with the gravel path, turn left and follow signs for the parking lot.

4.0 Arrive back at the trailhead.

16 Summit Lake State Park: Prairie Trail

Summit Lake State Park is the perfect depiction of a classic midwestern landscape. Corn and soybean fields give way to mature hardwood forests, lakeside views, marshland, and wide prairies. The Prairie Trail provides all of that plus a few Bald Eagle sightings if you're lucky. Its mild terrain and tranquil scenery are ideal for those seeking to decompress in nature.

Distance: 2.3-mile lollipop
Hiking time: 1–1.5 hours
Difficulty: Easy due to mild hilly terrain
Trail surface: Mostly grass path, some singletrack dirt sections
Best season: Spring or fall for bald eagle sightings and mid-summer for prairie flowers
Other trail users: Joggers, bird watchers
Canine compatibility: Leashed dogs permitted

Fees and permits: Entrance fee charged
Schedule: Daily from 7 a.m. to 11 p.m., year-round
Maps: Available at the entrance gate
Trail contact: Summit Lake State Park, 5993 N Messick Rd., New Castle 47362; (765) 766-5873; https://www.in.gov/dnr/parklake/2967.htm

Finding the trailhead: From Indianapolis take I-70 E. Continue for 39.4 miles, then take exit 123 for IN 3 N toward New Castle. Continue on IN 3 N for 11.1 miles, then turn right onto US 36 E. After 3.9 miles turn left onto Messick Road. The park entrance will be at the end of Messick Road. Just after the entrance gate, turn right onto the main north-south park road. The trailhead parking area will be located on the second right turn. GPS: N40 1.52' / W85 18.16'

The Hike

The Prairie Trail is the longest and most popular hike within Summit Lake State Park. It begins in an open area, offering a distant glimpse of the 800-acre reservoir to the north. Soon the trail enters the largest wooded area in the park. A singletrack trail will guide hikers through a rolling forest of oak-hickory, cherry, and a beech-maple mix as it flirts with the edge of the reservoir. Eventually the forest will give way to the outer edges of the prairie offering scenic lake views in one direction and a serene prairie landscape in the other. This is a great place to scan the skies for various raptor species such as red-tailed hawks, ospreys, and bald eagles. As you navigate through the prairie, various offshoots into the tall grass may tempt an unplanned adventure. While exploration is encouraged, be sure to stay on established trails in order to preserve this unique area. The lucky hikers who visit this trail during the prairie flower bloom will walk away with an unforgettable experience. As the trail follows the loop, it nears a marshland area around mile 1.4 where hikers may catch a glimpse of various waterfowls such as mallards. Shortly thereafter, you'll travel back into the forest toward the trailhead.

History

Summit Lake opened in 1985 and became Indiana's nineteenth state park in 1988. During this time, the park's 60-acre prairie was essentially a pasture as it was previously part of a farm. Overrun with invasive species like Canada thistle, the park mowed the fields and sprayed herbicide to battle the non-native plants in 1994 to basically start from scratch. Afterward the park planted an assortment of native grasses

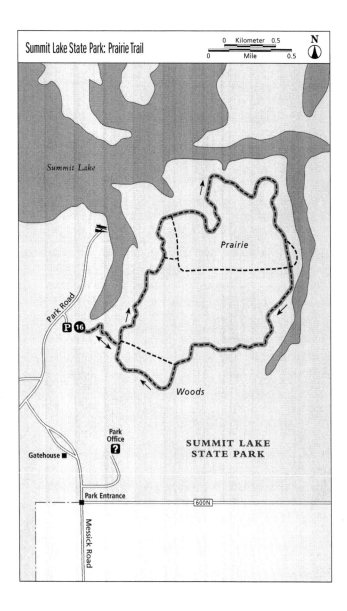

Summit Lake State Park: Prairie Trail

0   Kilometer   0.5

0   Mile   0.5

N

Summit Lake

Prairie

Park Road

P 16

Woods

Park
Office

Gatehouse

SUMMIT LAKE
STATE PARK

Park Entrance

600N

Messick Road

and prairie flowers which helped return the once decrepit pasture to its original glory. The park actively manages the invasive species issue by annually burning the prairie, which eradicates non-natives while not damaging the other prairie plants. In fact, the burning actually helps rejuvenate the soil resulting in healthier prairie grasses and flowers.

Miles and Directions

0.0 Start from the Prairie Trail parking lot, near the northern boat ramp.

0.1 Stay left at the T junction with the wooden Trail 1 marker, which will take you on the clockwise route.

0.4 Stay left at the two-way junction for the main trail. (**Option:** Going right will lead you into a system of unmarked trails that crisscross the prairie, eventually returning to the main trail at mile 0.5 and mile 1.4.)

0.5 At the four-way intersection, where you'll reach the opening of the main prairie, continue straight for the main trail.

0.7 Stay left at the unmarked trail junction.

1.2 Continue straight at the two-way junction to remain on the main trail. (**Option:** Turning left will put you on a brief detour that runs closer to the backwater marsh area and returns you to the main trail at mile 1.4.)

1.8 Continue straight at this T junction. (**Option:** Turning right leads to a shortcut through the forest, meeting back up with the main trail at mile 2.2.)

2.2 Here you'll exit the woods and reach the previously passed Trail 1 marker. Stay left to return to the trailhead.

2.3 Arrive back at the trailhead.

17 Mary Gray Bird Sanctuary

The 700-acre Mary Gray Bird Sanctuary is home to 6.5 miles of trails amongst gentle hills. This route combines three of the sanctuary's hikes, offering a mature forest, wetlands, and a hilltop meadow experience. You'll have the opportunity to spot over 60 bird species, 200 wildflower species, and multiple fern species during your visit. This hidden gem is sure to be the highlight of your weekend adventure.

Distance: 2.3-mile loop
Hiking time: 1.5-2 hours
Difficulty: Moderate due to some hilly terrain
Trail surface: Singletrack natural surface
Best season: Spring and fall for bird migration and seasonal changes
Other trail users: None
Canine compatibility: Leashed dogs permitted
Fees and permits: None, donations welcome

Schedule: Daily from dawn to dusk, year-round
Maps: Available at the kiosk and registration box near the shelter house
Trail contact: Mary Gray Bird Sanctuary, 3499 S Bird Sanctuary Rd., Connersville 47331; (765) 827-5109; https://indianaaudubon.org/places/united-states/indiana/connersville/birding-guide/mary-gray-bird-sanctuary

Finding the trailhead: From Indianapolis take I-465 E to I-74 E. Continue on I-74 E for 22 miles. Take exit 116 for IN 44 toward Shelbyville. Follow IN 44 E for 11 miles, then turn right onto South County Road 525 W. In 0.7 mile turn left onto West County Road 150 S and continue for another 0.7 mile. Turn right onto South Bird Sanctuary Road/County Road 450 W. In 2.2 miles, turn right at West

County Road 350 S. The park will be at the end of the road. The parking area will be on your right. GPS: N39 35.38' / W85 13.51'

The Hike

Like many of Indiana's hidden gems, the Mary Gray Bird Sanctuary is cloaked by the expanse of surrounding farmland. Its remote location means that the sanctuary is a great place to escape the crowds of Indiana's more popular natural areas. The sanctuary is owned and operated by the Indiana Audubon Society, which reserves some activities (such as camping and fishing) for its members but keeps their hiking areas open to the public. This moderate loop starts off on the Tulip Poplar Trail (Trail 3), and connects to the Woods Loop (Trail 9) and Beech (Trail 2) Trails. After leaving the parking area, the trail passes the Markel Barn on the left and moves between the first and second pond before turning right to follow the eastern bank of the second pond. Following signs for Trail 3, the path weaves through the hilliest section of the loop, crossing over several footbridges while climbing in and out of ravine bottoms. Be sure to look out for the trail's namesake of tulip poplar trees within the surrounding old growth forest. Around the 1-mile mark, Trail 3 ends as it meets the service road. Turn left onto the service road to continue on Trail 9. At mile 1.1 the trail turns right onto a singletrack trail and continues into the valley below. At mile 1.3 hikers will stay right for the connection trail to meet up with Trail 2. About a half mile into Trail 2, it crests the hill into Perkins Meadow where it passes a shelter on the left. This is a great area to watch for birds like the blue-winged warbler, scarlet tanager, and various hummingbird species. After staying left past the next two trail junctions, you'll descend the hill and reenter the forest. The trail will pass behind a private property area; be sure to respect the residence's privacy as you loop south back toward the trailhead.

History

In 1943, Alice Gray donated 264 acres of the sanctuary to the Indiana Audubon Society in memory of her late daughter, Mary. In 1947, Alice's husband, Finly Gray, a Democratic congressman from Connersville, bequeathed additional property to the society. Since then, member donations have allowed even more additions to the sanctuary's acreage.

Miles and Directions

0.0 Start from the parking lot, heading toward the red Markel Barn. Walk across the dam between the first and second ponds and then turn right, following the bank of the second pond going south.

0.2 At the footbridge near the third pond, turn left onto Trails 3/5 (Tulip Poplar/Woodpecker Trails). Turn right after the bridge at the T intersection. Shortly after the trail will split again; stay straight moving along the creek for Trail 3 (Tulip Poplar Trail).

1.0 Turn left onto the service road (Trail 9) and continue uphill. Follow the arrows for Trail 9 as it leads you along the northern edge of the field.

1.1 Turn right, leaving the service road for a singletrack trail, heading downhill. This is the beginning of the Trail 9 loop.

1.3 Stay right on the Trail 9 spur that connects Trail 9 (Woods Loop) with Trail 2 (Beech Trail).

1.4 After the bridge, turn left at the T junction onto Trail 2 (Beech Trail).

1.8 At the shelter house, continue straight past the intersection for Trail 8 (Malus Trail).

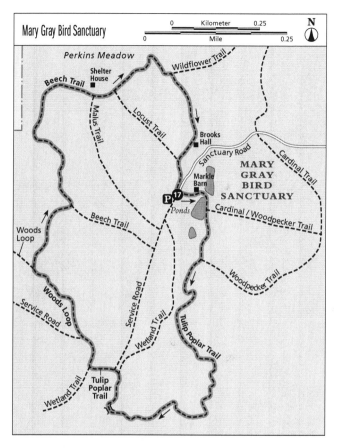

Mary Gray Bird Sanctuary

Kilometer 0.25
Mile 0.25

N

Perkins Meadow

Wildflower Trail

Beech Trail

Shelter House

Malus Trail

Locust Trail

Brooks Hall

Sanctuary Road

Cardinal Trail

MARY GRAY BIRD SANCTUARY

Markle Barn

P 17

Ponds

Cardinal / Woodpecker Trail

Beech Trail

Woods Loop

Woodpecker Trail

Service Road

Woods Loop

Service Road

Wetland Trail

Tulip Poplar Trail

Wetland Trail

Tulip Poplar Trail

1.9 Continue straight past the junction for Trail 10 (Locust Trail).

2.1 Before the bridge, turn right to stay on Trail 2 (Beech Trail).

2.2 You'll come to a house with a picket fence. Follow the trail around the fence and continue out into a field behind Brooks Hall, moving toward the parking lot.

2.3 Arrive back at the trailhead and parking lot.

18 Turkey Run State Park: Rocky Hollow-Falls Canyon Nature Preserve

The unique canyons of Turkey Run State Park are—debatably—the best hiking experience within Indiana. This route takes hikers through the most iconic features of the park including Boulder Canyon and the Punch Bowl. The narrow canyons, tall cliff faces, and various ladder climbs are sure to offer an unforgettable adventure.

Distance: 4.8-mile lollipop with double loops
Hiking time: 2.5–3 hours
Difficulty: More difficult due to length, hills, and rocky terrain
Trail surface: Natural surface singletrack with some gravel areas and canyon beds with some ladders
Best season: Spring for wild-flower bloom and waterfalls and fall for changing leaves
Other trail users: None

Canine compatibility: Leashed dogs permitted
Fees and permits: Entrance fee charged
Schedule: Open daily from 7 a.m. to 11 p.m., year-round
Maps: Available at entrance gate and Nature Center
Trail contact: Turkey Run State Park, 8121 E Park Rd., Marshall 47859; (765) 597-2635; https://www.in.gov/dnr/parklake/2964.htm

Finding the trailhead: From Indianapolis take I-465 N to I-74 W until you reach exit 52 for IN 75 toward Jamestown. Take a left onto IN 75 S and continue for 4.3 miles where the road will curve slightly to the left and become IN 234 W. Continue on IN 234 W for 16.6 miles before turning left onto IN 47 S. Follow IN 47 for 13.7 miles to

the Turkey Run State Park entrance on your right. Follow the signs to the Nature Center. GPS: N39 53.25' / W87 12.00'

The Hike

Caution: *Wet weather can make the sandstone canyons and wooden ladders dangerously slick and even impassable. Before setting out, check in at the Nature Center for trail conditions and closures.*

This stunning trail combines portions of Trails 3, 10, 5, and 9 to guide hikers through the most impressive features of the park. Starting behind the Nature Center, a well-traveled path leads down a stone staircase and toward the suspension bridge. Cross the bridge over Sugar Creek and into Rocky Hollow-Falls Canyon Nature Preserve—a 1,600-acre parcel of land within the park. Follow Trail 3 to the north after crossing the bridge. The trail will loop around into a wide canyon lined with towering cliffs. Around 0.3 mile you'll reach Wedge Rock, a massive, moss-covered boulder topped with a few brave trees. Soon, the canyon narrows and the path becomes a terrace of slick sandstone. The trail quickly reaches the Punch Bowl—a waterfall formed by pieces of rock that became trapped and swirled around by a backwash of glacial water, eventually producing a large pothole. Shortly thereafter the trail climbs a staircase that will connect with Trail 10. At mile 1.2 hikers will follow the Camel's Back spur to the right where the trail offers a view of the valley below. At 2.1 miles, after retracing the path back to Trail 10, the trail turns right. Step carefully as the trail descends three ladders into Bear Hollow. Upon exiting Bear Hollow turn right onto Trail 5, following Sugar Creek downstream. At 2.6 miles, Trail 5 meets Trail 9 where it turns right and ascends the stairs. Eventually, Trail 5 merges with Trail 9. At mile 3.2, Trail 9 descends into Boulder Canyon—named for the huge boulder field through which the trail winds. The trail climbs over a ridge and into Falls Canyon where it will reconnect with Trail 5. Follow the trail upstream past Ice Box and Crevice Rock where it crosses back over the bridge, toward the trailhead.

History

The sandstone gorges of Turkey Run State Park are 300 to 600 million years in the making. The exposed bedrock is called Mansfield sandstone and was formed during the Carboniferous Period. Sand from the mouth of the ancient Michigan River compacted and solidified over time. The sandstone was later carved into canyons by glacial melt during the Pleistocene Epoch period.

Miles and Directions

0.0 Start behind the Nature Center, moving toward Sugar Creek.

0.2 Cross the suspension bridge over Sugar Creek.

0.3 After the suspension bridge, turn right onto Trail 3 and cross a small footbridge into Rocky Hollow.

0.5 Continue straight for Trail 3 at the junction with Trail 4.

0.7 After climbing the stairs out of Rocky Hollow, turn right onto a Trail 10 connector.

1.2 At the T, where the trail becomes gravel, turn right onto a spur for Camel's Back.

1.3 Once reaching the Camel's Back, turn around and continue on the gravel Trail 10 heading south.

1.8 At the four-way intersection turn right onto Trail 3, heading downhill.

2.1 Climb down the ladders into Bear Hollow and continue straight past the Trail 5 connector on the right. Watch your step in this section and don't stand too close to the sandstone ledges.

2.3 At the T junction, marking the end of Bear Hollow, turn right onto Trail 5.

2.6 Stay right for Trail 5 at the three-way intersection with Trail 9.

Turkey Run State Park: Rocky Hollow-Falls Canyon Nature Preserve

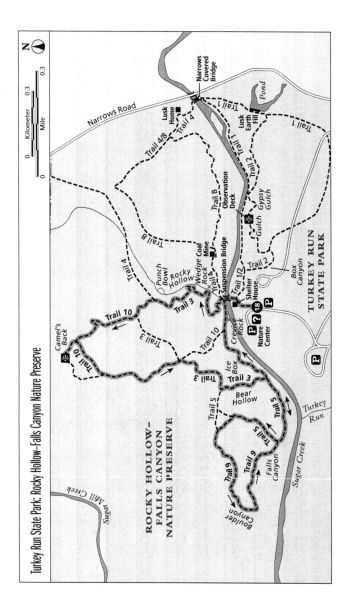

2.8 Continue straight past the two consecutive trail junctions on the right. As you continue Trail 5 will become Trail 9.

3.9 At the T junction, turn right for Trail 5, following Sugar Creek upstream toward the suspension bridge.

4.3 Pass Ice Box Canyon on the left.

4.6 Pass Crevice Rock and turn right onto the suspension bridge, moving back toward the trailhead and Nature Center.

4.8 Arrive back at the trailhead.

19 Hoosier National Forest: Pate Hollow

This 6.3-mile trail rewards hikers with stunning views of Lake Monroe at the loop's southernmost point. Moving through a diverse hardwood forest, hikers will experience the peaceful rolling hills of Indiana's only national forest.

Distance: 6.3-mile loop
Hiking time: 2.5-3.5 hours
Difficulty: More difficult due to length and hilly terrain
Trail surface: Natural surface singletrack
Best season: Fall for changing leaves
Other trail users: Joggers, hunters
Canine compatibility: Leashed dogs permitted
Fees and permits: None

Schedule: No restrictions
Maps: Available at trailhead and at the Paynetown State Recreation Area Office, 4850 S IN 446, Bloomington
Trail contact: Hoosier National Forest, 811 Constitution Ave., Bedford 47421; (812) 275-5987; https:// www.fs.usda.gov/recarea/ hoosier/recreation/hiking/ recarea/?recid=41584&actid=51

Finding the trailhead: From Indianapolis, take IN 37 S for 25.5 miles until it becomes I-69 S. Continue on I-69 S for 12.7 miles, then take exit 123 for Walnut Street/College Avenue. Continue onto North State Road 37 Business/North Walnut Street for 7.4 miles. Turn left onto State Road 46 E. After 2.8 miles, turn left onto East 3rd Street and continue for 1.4 miles. Turn left onto IN 446 S and continue to the Paynetown State Recreation Area Office on the right. The trailhead is behind the office at the northwest corner of the parking lot. GPS: N39 05.56' / W86 25.47'

The Hike

This 6.3-mile trail follows the outermost loop within the Pate Hollow Trail system. At both the beginning and end, the trail leads down ravines and over ridges, and is exhausting at times. However, the ridgetop section in the middle of the loop provides a much-needed break with quality views. The parking area for this trail is on Indiana DNR property, but you enter Hoosier National Forest shortly after the trail begins. The path quickly descends into a thick hollow and climbs the other side before connecting to the fire road for a brief period. It follows a forested ridgetop offering far off views of the rolling hills. Around mile 2.2 the trail begins to get peaking views of Lake Monroe. For about 1 mile, hikers follow the ridge as the lake views become wider and even more scenic. The trail comes closest to the lake shore just before climbing a series of switchbacks that'll lead away from the water and back toward the trailhead. A series of slight rights will lead hikers over two more ridges, through a mixed hardwood forest, and back toward the trailhead.

History

The hills of what is now Hoosier National Forest were once barren due to the overharvesting of lumber by the early 1900s. In the years leading up to and during the Great Depression, many landowners in the area abandoned their property as a way to cut their losses. In 1935, the Hoosier National Forest was created by Congress and rehabilitation efforts began by the Civilian Conservation Corps. Today, the forest comprises almost half of Indiana's public forest land, encompasses over 200,000 acres, and hosts over 260 miles of multi-use trails.

Hoosier National National Forest: Pate Hollow

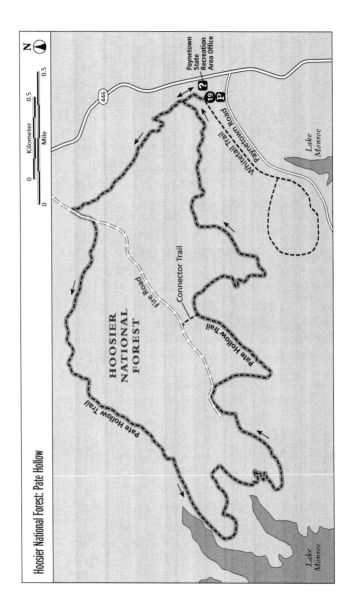

Paynetown State Recreation Area Office

446

Connector Trail

File Road

HOOSIER NATIONAL FOREST

Pate Hollow Trail

Pate Hollow Trail

Whitetail Trail

Paynetown Road

Lake Monroe

Lake Monroe

N

Kilometer   0.5

Mile   0.5

Miles and Directions

0.0   Start from the trailhead located behind the Recreation Area Office. Shortly thereafter, continue straight on the Pate Hollow Trail, passing the Whitetail Trail on the left.

0.1   Stay right at the split for a counterclockwise loop.

0.9   Where the singletrack Ts into an old forest road, take a left.

1.0   Follow the singletrack off to the right where it splits away from the old forest road and onto a singletrack trail. (**Option:** Continue on the forest service road to cut the distance almost in half.)

3.9   After the singletrack trail turns into a doubletrack, the trail will come to a split. Turn right at the split.

4.6   Turn right at the fork, moving toward the trailhead.

6.2   Stay right at the fork, continuing toward the trailhead.

6.3   Arrive back at the trailhead.

Clubs and Trail Groups

Indiana Audubon Society
3499 S. Bird Sanctuary Rd.
Connersville, IN 47331
(765) 827-5109; indianaaudubon.org
The Indiana Audubon Society aims to educate the public about birds and the protections they need as well as to protect and serve all natural resources of the region. Membership fees apply.

Central Indiana Wilderness Club
PO Box 781494
Indianapolis, IN 46278
ciwclub.org
Founded in 1982, the Central Indiana Wilderness Club offers wilderness adventures in Indiana and across the country through various activities. Membership fees apply.

Hoosier Hikers Council
PO Box 1327
Martinsville, IN 46151
(855) 812-4453; hoosierhikerscouncil.org
Founded in 1995, the Hoosier Hikers Council builds and improves Indiana trails. Membership fees apply.

Indianapolis Hiking Club
indyhike.org
Founded in 1957, the Indianapolis Hiking Club has more than 500 members. The club offers hikes year-round and of all different types.

Friends of Sugar Creek
PO Box 29
Crawfordsville, IN 47933
friendsofsugarcreek.org
The nonprofit's mission is to "protect, restore, and promote appreciation of Sugar Creek and its watershed." The organization has been operating for 30 years and hosts a variety of events.

Sierra Club
Hoosier Chapter
sierraclub.org/indiana
Founded in 1982, the Sierra Club is the country's oldest grassroots environmental organization. The Heartland Group of the Hoosier Chapter serves the greater Indianapolis area. Their website has local area information for meeting times. Membership fees apply.

Eagle Creek Foundation
(317) 327-7116; eaglecreekpark.org
Founded in 1978, the nonprofit was established to protect and improve Eagle Creek Park.

Friends of Brown County State Park
PO Box 1892
Nashville, IN 47448
(812) 988-5240; friendsbcsp.org
The organization's mission is the "conservation, education, preservation, research, and interpretation of Brown County State Park." Membership fees apply.

About the Authors

Kat Green and Kayla Woodward are both Indiana natives who bonded over their love of the outdoors during their time at Ball State University. Kayla, originally from McCordsville, spent much of her childhood around Fort Harrison State Park and other nearby natural areas. She earned a bachelor's and master's degree in telecommunications and digital storytelling, respectively, and much of her career has centered around elevating the voices and stories of indigenous people. Her personal and professional endeavors have taken her to natural areas across the country, including rain-soaked backpacking trips in Hoosier National Forest and dry desert hikes through the canyons of the Colorado Plateau.

Kat Green, raised in New Castle, found her love of the outdoors at a young age while trailing after her dad in the forests near her home. After earning a bachelor's degree in video production, she travelled seasonally across the country as a photographer and videographer for outdoor industries such as whitewater rafting and conservation organizations. During this time in her life, Kat not only expanded her hiking experience, but also found enjoyment in snowboarding, rock climbing, and various downriver sports. Now, as a freelance photographer residing in Washington State, Kat finds herself on the trail nearly every day.

THE TEN ESSENTIALS OF HIKING

American Hiking Society

Whether you plan to be gone for a couple of hours or several months, make sure to pack these items. Become familiar with these items and know how to use them.

Find other helpful resources at AmericanHiking.org/hiking-resources

1. **Appropriate Footwear**

2. **Navigation**

3. **Water** (and a way to purify it)

4. **Food**

5. **Rain Gear & Dry-Fast Layers**

6. **Safety Items** (light, fire, and a whistle)

7. **First Aid Kit**

8. **Knife or Multi-Tool**

9. **Sun Protection**

10. **Shelter**

PROTECT THE PLACES YOU LOVE TO HIKE

Become a member today and take $5 off an annual membership using the code **Falcon5**.

AmericanHiking.org/join

American Hiking Society is the only national nonprofit organization dedicated to empowering all to enjoy, share, and preserve the hiking experience.